SURVIVAL
WEAPONS

A User's Guide to the Best Self-Defense Weapons for Surviving Any Dangerous Situation

SAMMY FRANCO

Also by Sammy Franco

Knockout: The Ultimate Guide to Sucker Punching
Cane Fighting: The Authoritative Guide to Using the Cane or Walking Stick for Self-Defense
Kubotan Power: Quick & Simple Steps to Mastering the Kubotan Keychain
The Widow Maker Compendium
Invincible: Mental Toughness Techniques for Peak Performance
Bruce Lee's 5 Methods of Attack
Unleash Hell: A Step-by-Step Guide to Devastating Widow Maker Combinations
Feral Fighting: Advanced Widow Maker Fighting Techniques
The Widow Maker Program: Extreme Self-Defense for Deadly Force Situations
Savage Street Fighting: Tactical Savagery as a Last Resort
Heavy Bag Workout
Heavy Bag Combinations
Heavy Bag Training
The Complete Body Opponent Bag Book
Stand and Deliver: A Street Warrior's Guide to Tactical Combat Stances
Maximum Damage: Hidden Secrets Behind Brutal Fighting Combinations
First Strike: End a Fight in Ten Seconds or Less!
The Bigger They Are, The Harder They Fall
Self-Defense Tips and Tricks
Gun Safety: For Home Defense and Concealed Carry
Out of the Cage: A Guide to Beating a Mixed Martial Artist on the Street
Warrior Wisdom: Inspiring Ideas from the World's Greatest Warriors
War Machine: How to Transform Yourself Into a Vicious and Deadly Street Fighter
1001 Street Fighting Secrets
When Seconds Count: Self-Defense for the Real World
Killer Instinct: Unarmed Combat for Street Survival
Street Lethal: Unarmed Urban Combat

Survival Weapons: A User's Guide to the Best Self-Defense Weapons for Surviving Any Dangerous Situation
Copyright © 2017 by Sammy Franco
ISBN: 978-1-941845-41-7

Printed in the United States of America
Published by Contemporary Fighting Arts, LLC.
Visit us Online at: **SammyFranco.com**
Follow him on Twitter: **@RealSammyFranco**

Contents

"Our security is not a matter of weapons alone. The arm that wields them must be strong, the eye that guides them clear, the will that directs them indomitable."

– Franklin D. Roosevelt

Caution!

The self-defense techniques, tactics, weapons, and information described and depicted in this book can be dangerous and could result in serious injury and or death and should not be used or practiced in any way without the guidance of a qualified combat instructor.

The author, publisher, and distributors of this book disclaim any liability from loss, injury, or damage, personal or otherwise, resulting from the information and procedures in this book. This book is for academic study only.

Before you begin any exercise program, including those suggested in this book, it is important to check with your physician to see if you have any condition that might be aggravated by strenuous activity or exercise.

Remember, it's your sole responsibility to research and comply with all local, state and federal laws and regulations pertaining to the use of self-defense weapons and the application of self-defense techniques.

About This Book

Survival Weapons: A User's Guide to the Best Self-Defense Weapons for Any Dangerous Situation is a concise guide designed to introduce you to the best personal protection weapons. This practical, no-nonsense book is ideal for anyone who wants to learn how to arm themselves with the best self-defense weapons for real world survival situations.

The unique survival weapons featured in this book are low profile (practically invisible to the public) and can easily be concealed and carried on your person (legally permitting), in your vehicle, or carried in your survival bags. Best of all, they can be readily used in a broad range of environments - from the great outdoors to the city streets. By the way, when I say "survival bags" I am referring to the following three types. They include: everyday carry bag (EDC), get home bag (GHB), bug out bag (BOB).

Most of the self-defense weapons featured in this book are ubiquitous and can be readily used by young and old, regardless of size or strength and level of experience. Most importantly, you don't need martial arts training to master many of these devastating survival weapons.

Unlike other weapon related books, Survival Weapons: A User's Guide to the Best Self-Defense Weapons for Any Dangerous Situation is devoid of unreliable and gimmicky weapons that can get you injured or possibly killed when faced with a real-world self-defense crisis. Instead, this book arms you with the most efficient, effective, and practical tools that work in the chaos of a violent confrontation. In fact, the self-defense skills and techniques found within these pages are straightforward and easy to apply.

Practitioners who regularly practice the skills and techniques featured in this book will establish a rock solid foundation for using survival weapons. Moreover, the techniques featured in this book will significantly improve your overall self-defense skills, enhance your conditioning, and introduce you to a new and exciting method of personal protection.

This unique book is based on my 30+ years of research, training and teaching reality-based self-defense and combat sciences. In fact, I've taught these unique fighting weapons to thousands of my students, and I'm confident they can help protect you and your loved ones during an emergency self-defense situation.

I also encourage you to read this book from beginning to end, chapter by chapter. Only after you have read the entire book should you treat it as a reference and skip around, reading those chapters that directly apply to you

Finally, the information, techniques, and suggestions contained herein are dangerous and should only be used to protect yourself or a loved one from the immediate risk of unlawful injury. Remember, the decision to use a self-defense weapon must always be a last resort, after all other means of avoiding violence have been exhausted.

Be safe!

Sammy Franco

Introduction
Contemporary Fighting Arts

Welcome to Contemporary Fighting Arts

Before jumping into the book, I'd like to first introduce you to my unique system of self-defense called Contemporary Fighting Arts.

Contemporary Fighting Arts® (CFA), is a state-of-the-art combat system that was introduced to the world in 1983. This sophisticated and practical system of self-defense is designed specifically to provide efficient and effective methods to avoid, defuse, confront, and neutralize both armed and unarmed assailants in a variety of deadly situations and circumstances.

Unlike karate, kung-fu, mixed martial arts and the like, CFA is the first offensive-based combat system that is specifically designed for the violence that plagues our cruel city streets. CFA dispenses with the extraneous and the impractical and focuses on real-life self-defense.

Every tool, technique and tactic found within the CFA system must meet three essential criteria for fighting: efficiency, effectiveness, and safety. Efficiency means that the techniques permit you to reach your combative objective quickly and economically. Effectiveness means that the elements of the system will produce the desired effect. Finally, Safety means that the combative elements provide the least amount of danger and risk for you - the self-defense practitioner.

CFA is not about mind-numbing tournaments or senseless martial arts competition. It does not require you to waste time and energy practicing forms (katas) or other impractical rituals. There are no theatrical kicks or exotic techniques. Finally, CFA does not adhere blindly to tradition for tradition's sake. Simply put, it is a scientific yet pragmatic approach to staying alive in our world.

CFA has been taught to people of all walks of life. Some include the U.S. Border Patrol, police officers, deputy sheriffs, security guards, military personnel, private investigators, surgeons, lawyers, college professors, airline pilots, as well as black belts, boxers, and kick boxers. CFA's broad appeal results from its ability to teach people how to really fight.

It's All In The Name!

Before discussing the three components that make up Contemporary Fighting Arts, it is important to understand how CFA acquired its unique name. To begin, the first word, "Contemporary," was selected because it refers to the system's modern, up-to-date orientation. Unlike traditional martial arts, CFA is specifically designed to meet the challenges of our modern world.

The second term, "Fighting," was chosen because it accurately describes the system's combat orientation. After all, why not just call it Contemporary Martial Arts? There are two reasons for this. First, the word "martial" conjures up images of traditional and impractical martial art forms that are antithetical to the system. Second, why dilute a perfectly functional name when the word "fighting" defines the system so succinctly? Contemporary Fighting Arts is about teaching people how to really fight.

Let's look at the last word, "Arts." In the subjective sense, "art" refers to the combat skills that are acquired through arduous study, practice, and observation. The bottom line is that effective self-defense skills will require consistent practice and attention. Take, for example, something as seemingly basic as an elbow strike, which will actually require hundreds of hours of practice to perfect.

The pluralization of the word "Art" reflects CFA's protean instruction. The various components of CFA's training (i.e., firearms training, stick fighting, ground fighting, natural body weapon mastery, and so on) have all truly earned their status as individual art forms and, as such, require years of consistent study and practice to perfect. To acquire a greater understanding of CFA, here is an overview of the system's three vital components: the physical, the mental, and the spiritual.

The Physical Component

The physical component of CFA focuses on the physical development of a fighter, including combat conditioning, weapon and technique mastery, and self-defense attributes.

Combat Conditioning

If you are going to prevail in a combat situation, you must be physically fit. It's that simple. In fact, you will never master the tools and skills of combat unless you're in excellent physical shape. On the average, you will have to spend more than an hour a day to achieve maximum fitness.

In CFA combat conditioning comprises the following three broad components: cardiorespiratory conditioning, muscular/skeletal conditioning, and proper body composition.

The cardiorespiratory system includes the heart, lungs, and circulatory system, which undergo tremendous stress during the course of an altercation. So you're going to have to run, jog, bike, swim, or skip rope to develop sound cardiorespiratory conditioning. Each aerobic workout should last a minimum of 30 minutes and be performed at least four times per week.

The second component of combat conditioning is muscular/skeletal conditioning. In the world of self-defense, the strong survive and the rest go to the morgue. To strengthen your bones and muscles to withstand the rigors of a real fight, your program must include progressive resistance (weight training) and calisthenics. You will also need a stretching program designed to loosen up every muscle group. You can't kick, punch, ground fight, or otherwise execute the necessary body mechanics if you're "tight" or inflexible. Stretching on a regular basis will also increase the muscles' range of motion, improve circulation, reduce the possibility of injury, and relieve daily stress.

The final component of combat conditioning is proper body composition: simply, the ratio of fat to lean body tissue. Your diet and training regimen will affect your level or percentage of body fat significantly. A sensible and consistent exercise program accompanied by a healthy and balanced diet will facilitate proper body composition. Do not neglect this important aspect of physical fitness.

Weapon and Technique Mastery

You won't stand a chance against a vicious assailant if you don't master the weapons and tools of fighting. In CFA, we teach our students both armed and unarmed methods of combat. Unarmed fighting requires that you master a complete arsenal of natural body weapons and techniques. In conjunction, you must also learn the various stances, hand positioning, footwork, body mechanics, defensive structure, locks, chokes, and various holds. Keep in mind that something as simple as a basic punch will actually require hundreds of hours to perfect.

Range proficiency is another important aspect of weapon and technique mastery. Briefly, range proficiency is the ability to fight effectively in all three ranges of unarmed fighting. Although punching range tools are emphasized in CFA, kicking and grappling ranges cannot be neglected. Our kicking range tools consist of deceptive and powerful low-line kicks. Grappling range tools include head-butts, elbows, knees, foot stomps, biting, tearing, gouging, and crushing tactics.

Although CFA focuses on striking, we also teach our students a myriad of chokes, locks, and holds that can be used in a ground fight. While such grappling range submission techniques are not the most preferred methods of dealing with a ground fighting situation, they must be studied for the following six reasons: (1) level of force - many ground fighting situations do not justify the use of deadly force. In such instances, you must apply various non-lethal submission holds, (2) nature of the beast - in order to escape any choke, lock or hold, you must first know how to apply them yourself, (3) occupational requirement- some professional occupations (police, security, etc.) require that you possess a working knowledge of various submission techniques, (4) subduing a friend or relative - in many cases it is best to restrain and control a friend or relative with a submission hold instead of striking him with a natural body weapon, (5) anatomical orientation - practicing various chokes, locks and holds will help you develop a strong orientation of the human anatomy, and (6) refutation requirement - finally, if you are going to criticize the combative limitations of any submission hold, you better be sure that you can perform it yourself.

Defensive tools and skills are also taught. Our defensive structure is efficient, uncomplicated, and impenetrable. It provides the fighter maximum protection while allowing complete freedom of choice for acquiring offensive control. Our defensive structure is based on distance, parrying, blocking, evading, mobility, and stance structure. Simplicity is always the key.

Students are also instructed in specific methods of armed fighting. For example, CFA provides instruction about firearms for personal and household protection. We provide specific guidelines for handgun purchasing, operation, nomenclature, proper caliber, shooting fundamentals, cleaning, and safe storage. Our firearm program also focuses on owner responsibility and the legal ramifications regarding the use of deadly force.

CFA's weapons program also consists of natural body weapons, knives and edged weapons, single and double stick, makeshift weaponry, the side-handle baton, and oleoresin capsicum (OC) spray.

Combat Attributes

Your offensive and defensive tools are useless unless they are used strategically. For any tool or technique to be effective in a real fight, it must be accompanied by specific attributes. Attributes are qualities that enhance a particular tool, technique, or maneuver. Some examples include speed, power, timing, coordination, accuracy, non-telegraphic movement, balance, and target orientation.

CFA also has a wide variety of training drills and methodologies designed to develop and sharpen these combat attributes. For example, our students learn to ground fight while blindfolded, spar with one arm tied down, and fight while handcuffed.

Reality is the key. For example, in class students participate in full-contact exercises against fully padded assailants, and real weapon disarms are rehearsed and analyzed in a variety of dangerous scenarios. Students also train with a large variety of equipment, including heavy bags, double-end bags, uppercut bags, pummel bags, focus mitts, striking shields, mirrors, rattan sticks, foam and plastic bats, kicking pads, knife drones, trigger-sensitive (mock) guns, boxing and digit gloves, full-body armor, and hundreds of different environmental props.

There are more than two hundred unique training methodologies used in Contemporary Fighting Arts. Each one is scientifically designed to prepare students for the hard-core realities of real world combat. There are also three specific training methodologies used to develop and sharpen the fundamental attributes and skills of armed and unarmed fighting, including proficiency training, conditioning training, and street training.

Proficiency training can be used for both armed and unarmed skills. When conducted properly, proficiency training develops speed, power, accuracy, non-telegraphic movement, balance, and general psychomotor skill. The training objective is to sharpen one specific body weapon, maneuver, or technique at a time by executing it over and over for a prescribed number of repetitions. Each time the technique or maneuver is executed with "clean" form at various speeds. Movements are also performed with the eyes closed to develop a kinesthetic "feel" for the action. Proficiency training can be accomplished through the use of various types of equipment, including the heavy bag, double-end bag, focus mitts, training knives, real and mock pistols, striking shields, shin and knee guards, foam and plastic bats, mannequin heads, and so on.

Conditioning training develops endurance, fluidity, rhythm, distancing, timing, speed, footwork, and balance. In most cases, this type of training requires the student to deliver a variety of fighting combinations for three- or four-minute rounds separated by 30-second breaks. Like proficiency training, this type of training can also be performed at various speeds. A good workout consists of at least five rounds. Conditioning training can be performed on the bags with full-contact sparring gear, rubber training knives, focus mitts, kicking shields, and shin guards, or against imaginary assailants in shadow fighting.

Conditioning training is not necessarily limited to just three- or four-minute rounds. For example, CFA's ground fighting training can last as long as 30 minutes. The bottom line is that it all depends on what you are training for.

Street training is the final preparation for the real thing. Since many violent altercations are explosive, lasting an average of 20 seconds, you must prepare for this possible scenario. This means delivering explosive and powerful compound attacks with vicious intent for approximately 20 seconds, resting one minute, and then repeating the process.

Street training prepares you for the stress and immediate fatigue of a real fight. It also develops speed, power, explosiveness, target selection and recognition, timing, footwork, pacing, and breath control. You should practice this methodology in different lighting, on different terrains, and in different environmental settings. You can use different types of training equipment as well. For example, you can prepare yourself for multiple assailants by having your training partners attack you with focus mitts from a variety of angles, ranges, and target postures. For 20 seconds, go after them with vicious low-line kicks, powerful punches, and devastating strikes.

When all is said and done, the physical component creates a fighter who is physically fit and armed with a lethal arsenal of tools, techniques, and weapons that can be deployed with destructive results.

The Mental Component

The mental component of CFA focuses on the cerebral aspects of a fighter, developing killer instinct, strategic/tactical awareness, analysis and integration skills, philosophy, and cognitive skills.

The Killer Instinct

Deep within each of us is a cold and deadly primal power known as the "killer instinct." The killer instinct is a vicious combat mentality that surges to your consciousness and turns you into a fierce fighter who is free of fear, anger, and apprehension. If you want to survive the horrifying dynamics of real criminal violence, you must cultivate and utilize this instinctive killer mentality.

Survival Weapons

There are 14 characteristics of CFA's killer instinct. They are: (1) clear and lucid thinking, (2) heightened situational awareness, (3) adrenaline surge, (4) mobilized body, (5) psychomotor control, (6) absence of distraction, (7) tunnel vision, (8) fearless mind-set, (9) tactical implementation, (10) the lack of emotion, (11) breath control, (12) pseudospeciation, (13) viciousness, and (14) pain tolerance.

Visualization and crisis rehearsal are just two techniques used to develop, refine, and channel this extraordinary source of strength and energy so that it can be used to its full potential.

Strategic/Tactical Awareness

Strategy is the bedrock of preparedness. In CFA, there are three unique categories of strategic awareness that will diminish the likelihood of criminal victimization. They are criminal awareness, situational awareness, and self-awareness. When developed, these essential skills prepare you to assess a wide variety of threats instantaneously and accurately. Once you've made a proper threat assessment, you will be able to choose one of the following five self-defense options: comply, escape, de-escalate, assert, or fight back.

CFA also teaches students to assess a variety of other important factors, including the assailant's demeanor, intent, range, positioning and weapon capability, as well as such environmental issues as escape routes, barriers, terrain, and makeshift weaponry. In addition to assessment skills, CFA also teaches students how to enhance perception and observation skills.

Analysis and Integration Skills

The analytical process is intricately linked to understanding how to defend yourself in any threatening situation. If you want to be the best, every aspect of fighting and personal protection must be dissected. Every strategy, tactic, movement, and concept must be broken down to its atomic parts. The three planes (physical, mental, spiritual) of self-defense must be unified scientifically through arduous practice and constant exploration.

CFA's most advanced practitioners have sound insight and understanding of a wide range of sciences and disciplines. They include human anatomy, kinesiology, criminal justice, sociology, kinesics, proxemics, combat physics, emergency medicine, crisis management, histrionics, police and military science, the psychology of aggression, and the role of archetypes.

Analytical exercises are also a regular part of CFA training. For example, we conduct problem-solving sessions involving particular assailants attacking in defined environments. We move hypothetical attackers through various ranges to provide insight into tactical solutions. We scrutinize different methods of attack for their general utility in combat. We also discuss the legal ramifications of self-defense on a frequent basis.

In addition to problem-solving sessions, students are slowly exposed to concepts of integration and modification. Oral and written examinations are given to measure intellectual accomplishment. Unlike traditional systems, CFA does not use colored belts or sashes to identify the student's level of proficiency.

Philosophy

Philosophical resolution is essential to a fighter's mental confidence and clarity. Anyone learning the art of war must find the ultimate answers to questions concerning the use of violence in defense of himself or others. To advance to the highest levels of combat awareness, you must find clear and lucid answers to such provocative questions as could you take the life of another, what are your fears, who are you, why are you interested in studying Contemporary Fighting Arts, why are you reading this book, and what is good and what is evil? If you haven't begun the quest to formulate these important questions and answers, then take a break. It's time to figure out just why you want to know the laws and rules of destruction.

Cognitive Combat Skills

Cognitive combat exercises are also important for improving one's fighting skills. CFA uses visualization and crisis rehearsal scenarios to improve general body mechanics, tools and techniques, and maneuvers, as well as tactic selection. Mental clarity, concentration, and emotional control are also developed to enhance one's ability to call upon the controlled killer instinct.

The Spiritual Component

There are many tough fighters out there. In fact, they reside in every town in every country. However, most are nothing more than vicious animals that lack self-mastery. And self-mastery is what separates the true warrior from the eternal novice.

I am not referring to religious precepts or beliefs when I speak of CFA's spiritual component. Unlike most martial arts, CFA does not merge religion into its spiritual aspect. Religion is a very personal and private matter and should never, be incorporated into any fighting system.

CFA's spiritual component is not something that is taught or studied. Rather, it is that which transcends the physical and mental aspects of being and reality. There is a deeper part of each of us that is a tremendous source of truth and accomplishment.

In CFA, the spiritual component is something that is slowly and progressively acquired. During the challenging quest of combat training, one begins to tap the higher qualities of human nature. Those elements of our being that inherently enable us to know right from wrong and good from evil. As we slowly develop this aspect of our total self, we begin to strengthen qualities profoundly important to the "truth." Such qualities are essential to your growth through the mastery of inner peace, the clarity of your "vision," and your recognition of universal truths.

One of the goals of my system is to promote virtue and moral responsibility in people who have extreme capacities for physical and mental destructiveness. The spiritual component of fighting is truly the most difficult aspect of personal growth. Yet, unlike the physical component, where the practitioner's abilities will be limited to some degree by genetics and other natural factors, the spiritual component of combat offers unlimited potential for growth and development. In the final analysis, CFA's spiritual component poses the greatest challenges for the student. It is an open-ended plane of unlimited advancement.

Chapter 1
How to Improve Your Chances of Survival

Four Survival Concepts

Before jumping into the specific survival weapons, it's important first to cover a few essential topics that will significantly enhance your safety and survival during an emergency situation. They include the following:

- **Situational Awareness**
- **Threat Assessment**
- **Avoiding Excessive Force**
- **Controlling Fear**

Situational Awareness

Situational awareness is total alertness, presence, and focus on virtually everything in your immediate surroundings. You must train your senses to detect and assess the people, places, objects, and actions that can pose a danger to you. Do not think of situational awareness simply in terms of the five customary senses of sight, sound, smell, taste, and touch. In addition, the very real powers of instinct and intuition must also be developed and eventually relied upon.

Two vagrants congregating on the street corner or by your car, the stranger lingering at the mailboxes in your lobby, the delivery man at the door, a deserted parking lot, an alleyway near a familiar sidewalk, the stray dog ambling toward you in the park, a large limb hanging precariously from a tree . . . these are all obvious examples of persons, places, and objects that can pose a threat to you. Situational awareness need not - and should not - be limited to preconceived notions about obvious sources of danger.

Unfortunately, very few people have refined their situational awareness skills. The reasons are many. Some are in denial about the prevalence of criminal violence while others are too distracted by life's everyday problems and pressures to pay attention to the hidden dangers that lurk around them. Whatever the reasons, poor awareness skills can get you into serious trouble and could cost you your life.

During a SHTF situation, situational awareness is total alertness, presence, and focus on virtually everything in your immediate surroundings. You must train your senses to detect and assess the people, places, objects, and actions that can pose a danger to you.

Situational awareness, in terms of threats posed by human attackers, begins with an understanding of criminal psychology. It is a common misconception that criminals are stupid and incompetent. Although many may be uneducated by traditional standards, they are not stupid. On the contrary, they can be shrewd, methodical, bold, and psychologically dominant. The especially dangerous ones are often expert observers of human behavior, capable of accurately assessing your body language, walk, talk, carriage, state of mind, and a variety of other indicators. They know what to look for and how to exploit it.

Survival Weapons

Criminals are also selective predators. Many rapists, for example, will test a victim by engaging her in idle conversation, following her, or invading her space in some preliminary and seemingly harmless manner. Carefully selected measures designed to evaluate fear, apprehension, and awareness are part of the attacker's overall strategy. Seasoned criminal aggressors are looking for easy strikes - what they call the "vic." Chronic brawlers, street punks, and muggers operate in the same basic manner. They look for the weak, timid, disoriented, and unaware victims.

As you develop situational awareness, you transmit a different kind of signal to the enemy's radar. Weakness and uncertainty are replaced by confidence and strength. Your carriage and movements change. You will be seen as assertive and purposeful. You are less likely to be perceived as an easy mark or a "vic," and your chances of being attacked will significantly diminish.

Situational awareness also diminishes the potency of the criminal's favorite weapon—surprise. Your ability to foresee and detect danger will diminish his ability to stalk you, or lie in wait in ambush zones. Ambush zones are strategic locations from which criminal assailants launch their attacks. Every day millions of Americans walk through numerous ambush zones and never even know it. Ambush zones are everywhere. They can be found and exploited in unfamiliar and familiar environments, even in your home, and in unpopulated and populated areas. An ambush zone can be set in a dark or poorly lit area as well as in a well-lit area. An ambush zone can be established in a variety of common places: under, behind, or around trees, utility boxes, shrubs, beds, corners, dumpsters, doorways, walls, tables, cars, trash cans, rooftops, bridges, ramps, mailboxes, etc. They are everywhere!

In addition to enhancing your ability to detect, avoid, and strategically neutralize ambush zones, situational awareness allows you to detect and avoid threats and dangers not necessarily predicated on the element of surprise. Some situations afford potential victims the luxury of actually seeing trouble coming. Nonetheless, it's remarkable how many people fail to heed obvious signs of danger because of poor awareness skills. They overlook the signals—belligerence, furtiveness, hostility, restlessness—so often manifested by criminal attackers. They neglect the opportunity to cross the street long before the shoulder-to-shoulder encounter with a pack of young toughs moving up the sidewalk. Once it's too late to avoid the confrontation, a whole new range of principles comes

Ambush zones are everywhere, how many do you see in this photo?

quickly into play. The best defense is a heightened level of situational awareness. You must learn to avoid situations that will require the use of physical force, and the highest form of self-defense is being smart enough to avoid the encounter in the first place.

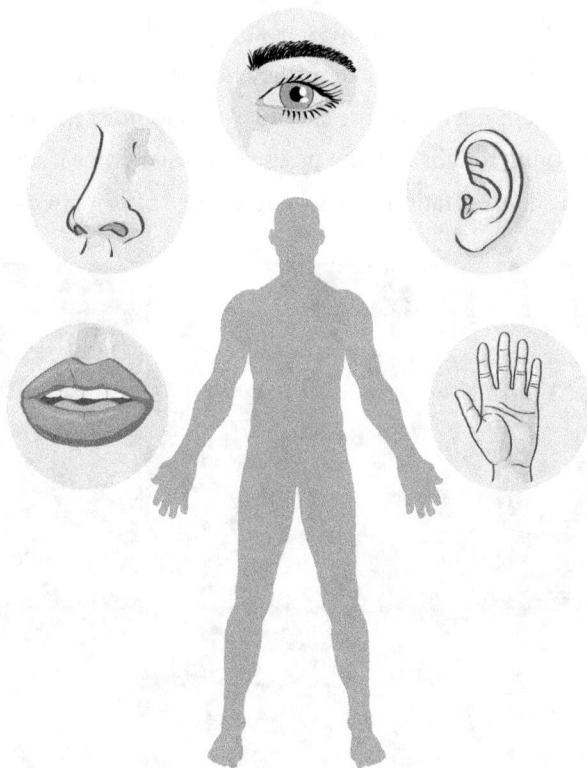

Situational awareness requires you to train all of your senses to detect and assess the people, places, objects, and actions that can pose a danger to you and your loved ones.

Situational Awareness Exercises

1. Detect five different ambush zones at your workplace and write them down. Don't pick the obvious ones. It's your life; learn to think like the criminal.

2. Detect five different ambush zones in front of your home. If you didn't find five, you didn't look hard enough.

3. Over the next ten days do not allow yourself to be taken by surprise—by anyone! Every time it happens, record the circumstances: who, what, when, how, where, and why.

4. When you watch television, go to the movies, look at pictures, or read books, note ambush zones that have not occurred to you in your other assessments. Note them in writing.

5. Visualize five different settings. They can be friendly and familiar like your backyard, or hostile and strange. Write down the things that you have mentally noted in these visualized settings.

Self Awareness

Self-awareness has been the subject of philosophers and mystics for centuries. Socrates said, "Know thyself." He believed self-knowledge to be essential to the attainment of true virtue.

Self-awareness is a critical component of self-defense, but what does it mean to know yourself? Of course, you know your tastes and preferences, your desires, your occupation, and so forth. But do you know who you really are? What aspects of your self provoke violence and which, if any, would promote a proper reaction in defense against a threat of violence to you or others? Let's look at certain aspects important to self-protection and ask ourselves a few tough questions.

Physical Attributes

What are your physical strengths and weaknesses? Are you overweight or underweight? Is your body language and the manner in which you carry yourself more likely to provoke or deter a violent attack? Do you have any training in self-defense? Are you fit or out of shape? Do you have the skill to disarm a knife-wielding attacker? Do you smoke or drink excessively? Are you skilled with firearms or edged weapons?

Mental Attributes

What are your mental strengths and weaknesses? Are you an optimist or pessimist? Can you summon up courage and confidence even when you are feeling fearful or insecure? How do you handle stress? Do you panic or frighten easily? Do you have any phobias? What are your fears? Do you think well on your feet?

Communication Skills

What are your strengths and weaknesses in expressing yourself with words? Are you likely to aggravate or diffuse a hostile situation? Are your words congruent with your tone of voice? Can you communicate adequately under stressful situations, or do you become nonplused?

Personality Traits

What type of person are you? Are you passive or aggressive? Are you opinionated and argumentative or open-minded and deliberative? Are you fiery, loud, and boisterous, or quiet, subdued, and calm? Are you quick to anger? Do you harbor grudges? Are there sensitive issues or remarks that may cause you to lose your temper?

Gender and Age

What are the different types of violent crimes that are directed toward you because of your sex? Women are much more likely than men to be raped or abused by their spouses. On the other hand, males are more apt than females to be victims of homicides. Is your age an open invitation for an attack? Children are more likely to be molested or kidnapped than adults, and older adults are weaker and more vulnerable to attack than middle-aged people.

Occupation

Does the nature of your occupation make you or your family vulnerable to different forms of criminal violence? Are you involved with the military or law enforcement? Are you a celebrity? Do you have diplomatic or political connections? Do you control large sums of money or valuable drugs? Does your political affiliation make you or your family a likely target for kidnapping and terrorism?

Income Level

What types of crime are directed toward you because of your income level? Are you wealthy, comfortable, or poor? Does your income level make you and your family vulnerable to kidnapping for ransom? Or does your financial situation force you and your family to live in poor neighborhoods that invite violent crime? Are you wealthy and flashy with outward evidence of this wealth?

Self-Awareness Exercises

The following questions were designed to start you thinking in the important process of self-awareness. Use them to form an overall personal profile of yourself. The goal is to recognize traits that provoke and/or prevent a violent attack.

1. Think of five physical and five mental weaknesses that would inhibit your survival in a self-defense situation.

2. Recall a very stressful situation. How did you react? How did you feel? Were you angry? Did you lose control? Were you calm, notwithstanding the pressure?

3. Ask a close friend or your spouse to evaluate your communication skills in a variety of situations with other people. Are you open and receptive, rude or polite, emphatic and expressive, or reserved and withdrawn? Do not react defensively to the critique you receive, even if you don't agree.

4. Look into the mirror and conjure up the following mental and emotional states, carefully noting your facial expressions as they arise: anger, happiness, sadness, depression, surprise, and fear.

5. Go back to the preceding exercise and focus on anger. Pay close attention to your facial expressions and other physiological manifestations. What do you see?

6. Think of three forms of violent crime that you may be subject to because of your lifestyle.

7. Think of three forms of violent crime that you may be subject to because of your gender.

8. To gain a better understanding of yourself, complete the following four exercises. Be frank and truthful.

- Do you believe you could take the life of another human being if you had to?

- List four of your greatest fears.

- What steps might you take to eliminate or diminish those fears?

- Name three issues, topics, comments, or situations that would provoke you to lose your temper.

What is Threat Assessment?

We assess many different things every day. For example, we assess such divergent things as shopping values, the pros and cons of career moves, and different aspects of our relationships with others. The requisite skills for these assessments vary, depending on the elements involved. Skills for assessing the effect of fluctuating interest rates on the stock market are very different from those necessary to assess the effect of a volcano on global weather patterns. The analytical processes may be similar, but the knowledge and skills need to be encountered individually, and not arbitrarily.

Similarly, in the world of self-defense, threat assessment is the process of rapidly gathering and analyzing information, then accurately evaluating it in terms of threat and danger. In general, you can assess people, places, objects, and actions. In addition, assessment skills require sharp perception and keen observation. Your perception skills can be heightened, and your ability to observe can be enhanced.

Threat assessment is the process of rapidly gathering and analyzing information, then accurately evaluating it in terms of threat and danger.

We gather information through our sensory processes. You see a movement in the shadows of your backyard. You hear footsteps approaching from behind you in a dark parking lot. You smell cigarette smoke in what you thought was a deserted area. You feel a breeze coming up your stairwell when all the doors and windows are supposed to be shut. You taste the sickening metallic flavor of fear in your mouth.

These five senses can be sharpened through a variety of exercises designed to develop both raw detection and learned identification capabilities. For example, sit alone in your backyard for a given period of time and catalog the various things your five senses detect. Next, list the possible sources of the sensory data. With practice, you will make remarkable progress from being unable to detect a particular sound or smell to not only detecting it quickly and accurately but also identifying its source. This development increases as these exercises are performed in different types of settings. Imagine, for example, the things you would hear, see, and smell on a dark night in the middle of a suburban park, as opposed to what you would experience standing in a dark urban alley. Remember, you are only limited by your imagination.

Additionally, you can also heighten your ability to observe. Have you ever noticed how keenly you study people, buildings, streets, signs, animals, and various other everyday things when you travel to a strange city or to another country? Watch a dog in a new environment, with its nose in the air and ears perked in alertness. People and animals tend to observe more actively in strange or new environments. This practice reveals an old survival process at work. Conversely, we tend to become less observant in familiar settings. We let our guard down, so to speak. For example, how many times has your wife or girlfriend changed her hair, or your husband or boyfriend shaved his beard, and you simply didn't notice it?

Here's the good news: observational skills can be expanded with application of an intelligent program. In my Contemporary Fighting Arts (CFA) self-defense system, students are instructed to practice quickly, memorizing lines of verse in a hectic setting. The turmoil around them can work to strengthen their concentration. In some situations students will practice studying scenes on the streets, trying to spot the threat or potential danger. It might be a suspicious man lurking in an alleyway, a group of restless youths congregating at a street corner, or a figure in a second-story window cradling what might be a high-powered rifle. These are just a few exercises to sharpen your self-defense and observational skills. Military and intelligence agencies are experts in this area of training.

Even though the senses can be sharpened and the powers of observation enhanced, the ability to process information varies with the individual. Two average untrained people who witness the same event are likely to report it differently. This is referred to as "individual perception." In part, previous experiences can determine the manner in which an individual will react to stimuli. People of different ages, cultures, or occupational backgrounds may see the same event very differently. The actual physical processes involved in perception are much the same in every person. But it is the manner in which data is interpreted that determines what a person sees. When it comes to self-defense, you must attempt to remove preconceived notions, assumptions, and biases that may lead to dangerously incorrect conclusions or oversights. These false reactions form actual blocks to your ability to grasp reality.

Choosing The Right Self-Defense Response

Accurate assessment is critical in self-defense for two reasons. First, it is imperative that you choose the most appropriate tactical response. There are five possible tactical responses to any particular self-defense situation, listed in order of increasing level of resistance:

- **Comply**
- **Escape**
- **De-escalate**
- **Assert**
- **Fight Back**

Accurate assessment skills will help you choose the appropriate response for the situation.

Comply means to obey the assailant's commands. For example, if you are held at gun point (out of disarming range) for the purpose of robbery, there is nothing to do but comply. Take out your wallet, take off your watch, hand over your car keys, do what you are told. Comply.

Escape or Tactical Retreat means to flee from the threat or danger safely and rapidly. For example, if you are being held hostage and your captor is distracted long enough for you to escape safely, then do it.

De-Escalate means the art and science of diffusing a hostile individual. Not every confrontation warrants fighting back. Often you will be able to use de-escalation skills to talk someone out of a possible violent encounter. An intoxicated loudmouth may be just the type of guy you can settle down and lead away from a problem with effective de-escalation skills.

Assert means standing up for you and your rights. Through effective communication skills you can thwart a person's efforts to intimidate, dominate, and control you. For example, let's say you're working late at the office and your boss makes sexual advances toward you. Now is the time to confront him and be assertive. In a firm and confidant manner, you tell him that you're not interested and that you want him to stop his offensive actions immediately.

Fight Back means using various physical and psychological tactics and techniques to stun, incapacitate, cripple or kill your attacker(s). For example, you're trapped in a dead-end alley by a knife-wielding psychotic who appears determined to butcher you. Your only option is to fight back!

These are just a few of the many possible examples of the five tactical responses. Every self-defense situation is different, and, moreover, most situations can be fluid. A dangerous situation might present an escape option at one moment but quickly turn into a fight-back situation at the next. For example, let's say that you are kidnapped and your captor leaves a door unlocked, and in your effort to escape, you run into him on your way out. Obviously, that is the time to fight for your life.

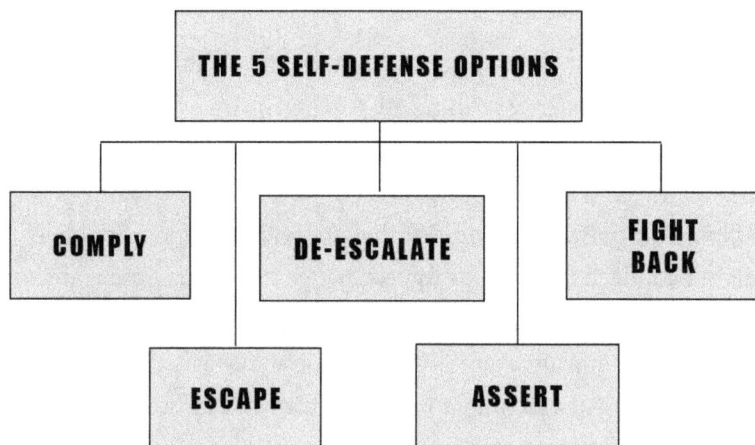

```
                    ┌──────────────────────────────┐
                    │  THE 5 SELF-DEFENSE OPTIONS   │
                    └──────────────────────────────┘

  ┌─────────┐        ┌──────────────┐        ┌───────────┐
  │ COMPLY  │        │ DE-ESCALATE  │        │   FIGHT   │
  │         │        │              │        │   BACK    │
  └─────────┘        └──────────────┘        └───────────┘

        ┌──────────┐           ┌──────────┐
        │  ESCAPE  │           │  ASSERT  │
        └──────────┘           └──────────┘
```

Avoiding Excessive Force

There is a second important reason why assessment skills are critical in self-defense: the law. There is an interesting irony facing all law enforcement officers, self-defense, and martial art experts. The more highly trained, knowledgeable, and better you are in firearms, knives, combat tactics, martial arts, and other self-defense skills, the higher the standard of care you must observe when protecting yourself or others. If you act too quickly or use what someone might consider "excessive force" in neutralizing an assailant, you may end up being a defendant in a legal process.

America is the most violent society on earth. It is also the most litigious. Most people do not realize that developing a deadly capability to protect yourself carries a tremendous moral and social responsibility. It also involves the risk of civil liability and criminal jeopardy. If you blind or cripple a person, you'd better be prepared to justify this act in the eyes of the law. If you're not careful, you could spend the rest of your life supporting the person who meant to harm you - assuming, of course, that you can get a job once you get out of jail!

The two most popular questions students ask after they have had a little self-defense training are when can you use physical force, and how much physical force is justified? Well, there are no simple answers to these questions. Again, every self-defense situation is different. In one case, a side kick that dislocates an attacker's knee might be judged appropriate force. Change the facts a little and you have a civil battery suit and a criminal charge of aggravated assault. Killing a criminal attacker in one situation may be justified, but a seemingly similar case might result in a civil suit for wrongful death and a criminal charge of manslaughter or murder.

The basic principle is that you must never use force against another person unless it is justified. For civilians, force is broken down into two broad categories: lethal and nonlethal. Any time you use physical force against another person, you run the risk of having a civil suit filed against you. Anyone can hire a lawyer and file a suit for damages. Likewise, anyone can file a criminal complaint against you. Whether criminal charges will be brought against you depends upon the prosecutor or grand jury's views of the facts. No two cases are the same, so there are no easy answers.

I am not qualified to be offering you legal advice. Frankly, I know enough about the law not to make that mistake. However, I can tell you that if you are a highly trained self-defense expert, you will be held to a higher standard of behavior by a jury of your peers. Now there's a good one for you - a jury of your peers. If I ever have to be on trial, I hope that the jury will be comprised of twelve trained self-defense experts. But I won't hold my breath.

A particular troublesome angle to self-defense and legal liability is my first-strike principle (FSP). In many cases, jurors will decide self-defense issues on who struck whom first. That's not good news. My rule is: when faced with a harmful or deadly force situation, and when danger is imminent, then strike first, strike fast, and strike with authority. The problem arises because you may have a hard time justifying your approach in the antiseptic and safe environment of a courtroom many months later. Whenever my life has been in imminent danger, I always acted swiftly. Whether you adopt this approach is entirely up to you.

When to Use Assessment Skills

You should always be alert. Don't become complacent and comfortable. Never assume there is no danger! Learn to assess the situation promptly and accurately, reach a rational conclusion, and choose the appropriate tactical response. The only time you should forget about assessment is when you've been attacked by surprise. For example, a mugger lunges from behind a car, grabs you by the throat, and throws you to the ground. Then it's too late for assessment skills. You must act intuitively and immediately to neutralize him, or you're going to be a statistic. Remember, time is of the essence, and your reaction and reflex must take the place of assessment.

What to Assess

There are two broad factors to assess in any self-defense situation: the environment and the individual(s). Let's first look at the environment and its related factors.

The Environment

In any self-defense situation you must strategically evaluate your environment, which is made up of your immediate surroundings. lt can be a parking lot, your car, your bedroom, your office, an airport, a park, elevator, nightclub, movie theater, etc. There are four essential factors to consider when assessing your environment. They are escape routes, barriers, makeshift weapons, and terrain. Let's take a look at each one.

Escape routes. These are the various avenues or exits from a threatening situation. There is nothing cowardly about running away from a dangerous situation. The ultimate goal of self-defense is to survive. Some possible escape routes are windows, doors, fire escapes, gates, escalators, fences, walls, bridges, and staircases. But be careful that your version of an escape route doesn't lead you into a worse situation.

Barriers. A barrier is any object that obstructs the attacker's path of attack. At the very least, barriers give you distance and some precious time, and they may give you some safety—at least temporarily. A barrier must have the structural integrity to perform the particular function you have assigned it. Barriers are everywhere and include such things as large desks, doors, automobiles, Dumpsters, large trees, fences, walls, heavy machinery, and large vending machines. The list is endless and depends on the situation, but it is a good idea to assess in advance any possible barriers when entering a potentially hostile or dangerous environment.

Makeshift weapons. These are common, everyday objects that can be converted into offensive and defensive weapons. Like a barrier, a makeshift weapon must be appropriate to the function you have assigned to it. You won't be able to knock someone out with a car antennae, but you could whip it across their eyes and temporarily blind them. Whereas you could knock someone unconscious with a good heavy flashlight but you could not use it to shield yourself from a knife attack.

Makeshift weapons can be broken down into four types: striking, distracting, shielding, and cutting weapons.

Striking makeshift weapons, as the name implies, are objects that can be used to strike an assailant. Examples include heavy flashlights, baseball bats, bottles, beer mugs, text books, binoculars, small lamps, hammers, pool cues, canes, umbrellas, vases, walking sticks, crowbars, light dumbbells, barstools, chairs, etc.

Distracting makeshift weapons are objects that can be thrown at the attacker(s) to temporarily distract him. Depending on the size of the object, a distraction weapon can be thrown into an assailant's face, body, or legs. They include car keys, glass bottles, rolled-up newspaper or magazine, text books, dirt, gravel, sand, hot liquids, spare change, ashtrays, paperweights, wallets, purses, and briefcases. Trash cans, chairs, and bicycles can also be kicked or slammed into an assailant's legs.

Shielding makeshift weapons are objects that temporarily shield you from the assailant's punch, kick, or strike. In some cases, shielding weapons can also be used to protect against knife and bludgeon attacks. Examples of shielding weapons include: trash can lids, briefcases, luggage bags, doors, sofa cushions, thick pillows, ironing boards, hubcaps, food trays, lawn chairs, small tables, backpack, etc.

Cutting makeshift weapons are objects that can be used to cut the assailant by either stabbing or slashing him. Examples include all kitchen cutlery, forks, screwdrivers, broken bottles, broken glass, scissors, car keys, pitch forks, ice scrapers, letter openers, pens, sharp pencils, razor blades, etc. Obviously there is some overlap between the various categories of make-shift weapons. For example, a briefcase can be thrown into an attacker's face for distraction, used to shield against a knife attack, or slammed into an assailant's temple to knock him out.

Terrain. This is a critical environmental factor. What are the strategic implications of the terrain that you are standing on? Will the surface area interfere with your ability to defend against an assailant? Is the terrain wet or dry, mobile or stationary? Obviously, if you are standing on ice, you will be restricted in your efforts to quickly escape or attempt kicking techniques. If the surface is shaky, like a suspension bridge, for example, you may be required to avoid kicking your assailant and instead fight back with hand techniques.

The Individual(s)

Obviously, in a potentially dangerous situation, you need to assess the source of the threat. Who is posing the possible danger? Is it someone you know or is he a complete stranger? Is it one person or two or more? What are his or her intentions in confronting you? Pay attention to all available clues, particularly verbal and nonverbal indicators. Let all five of your senses go to work to absorb the necessary information. Also don't forget to listen to what your gut instincts are telling you about the threatening person(s). There are five essential factors to consider when assessing a threatening individual: demeanor, intent, range, positioning, and weapon capability.

Demeanor. In the broadest terms we are talking about the individual's outward behavior. Watch for clues and cues. Is he shaking, or is he calm and calculated? Are his shoulders hunched or relaxed? Are his hands clenched? Is his neck taut? Are his teeth clenched? Is he breathing hard? Does he seem angry or frustrated, or confused and scared? Does he seem high on drugs? Is he mentally ill or simply intoxicated? What is he saying? How is he saying it? Is his speech slurred? What is his tone of voice? Is he talking rapidly or methodically? Is he cursing and angry? All of these verbal and nonverbal cues are essential in assessing the individual's overall demeanor and thus adjusting your tactical response accordingly.

Intent. Once you've got a good read on the assailant's demeanor, you're in a much better position to assess his or her intent. In other words, just what is this person's purpose in confronting you? Does he intend to rob you? Is he seeking retribution for something you have done? Or is he simply looking to pick a fight with you? Determining the individual's intent is perhaps the most important assessment factor, but it can also be the most difficult. Moreover, when it comes to criminal intent, things can change pretty quickly. For example, an intent to rob can quickly turn into an intent to rape. In any event, the appropriate tactical response is highly dependent upon a correct assessment of intent.

Range. Range is the spatial relationship between you and the assailant(s) in terms of distance. In self-defense there are three possible distances from which your assailant can launch an attack: Kicking range, Punching range, and Grappling range. Kicking range is the furthest range from which the attacker can kick you, lunge at you with or without a weapon, or strike you with a bludgeon. Punching range is the midrange from which the attacker can strike you with his hands, grab or push you, cut you with a knife, or strike you with a bludgeon. Grappling range is the closest range, from which the assailant can wrestle, grab, push, or choke you, and cut you with an edged weapon. When assessing a threatening individual, you'll need to recognize the strategic implications of his range. For example, how close is he from launching a punch? Is he at a distance from which he could kick you? Is he in a range that allows him to grab hold of you, take you to the ground, or cut you with an edged weapon? Is he moving through the ranges of unarmed combat? If so, how fast? Does he continue to move forward when you step back?

Positioning. This is the spatial relationship of the assailant(s) to you in terms of threat, escape, and target selection. Are you surrounded by multiple assailants or only one? Is he standing squarely or sideways, above or below you? What anatomical targets does the assailant present you with? Is he blocking the door or any other avenue of escape? Is his back to the light source? Is he close to your only makeshift weapon? You must answer these questions before choosing a tactical strategy appropriate to the situation.

Weapon capability. Is your assailant armed or unarmed? If he is carrying a weapon, what type is it? Does he have a delivery method for the particular weapon? Is he armed with more than one weapon? Sometimes it is easy to determine if someone is armed. For example, you see a knife sheath on his belt. At other times your assessment skills need to be more advanced. For example, is the person wearing a jacket when it is too hot for a jacket? Could it be to conceal a gun at the waist? Is the person patting his chest? When scanning the person, can you see his hands and all his fingertips? Is one hand behind him or in his pockets? Could he be palming a knife or some other edged weapon? Are his arms crossed? Does he seem to be reaching for something? Does he seem suspiciously rooted to a particular spot? Is his body language incongruous with his verbal cues you are reading? The CFA rule: When you're not certain, always assume your assailant is armed with a weapon.

Controlling Fear

To the untrained person, any kind of violent encounter will result in some level of fear. Fear is a strong and unpleasant emotional reaction to a real or perceived threat. If uncontrolled, fear leads to panic. Then it's too late to adequately protect yourself.

The Three Levels of Fear

To prevent the negative effects of fear, you need to understand its levels and dynamics. For analysis, I have categorized fear into three different levels, listed in order of intensity:

- **Fright (quick or sudden fear)**
- **Panic (overpowering fear)**
- **Terror (crippling or immobilizing fear)**

While these three levels of fear vary in degrees of stress, they all have one common root response: the fight-or-flight response.

What is The Fight-or-Flight Response?

Whenever a person, or any animal for that matter, feels threatened or frightened, certain physiological changes occur. They start in the brain when the hypothalamus sends strong impulses to the pituitary gland, causing it to release a hormone (ACTH) that stimulates the adrenal glands to release other hormones into the bloodstream.

Ultimately every nerve and muscle is involved. This adrenaline will cause an increased heart rate with a corresponding increase in respiration and blood pressure. Your muscles will tense up, you will start to sweat, and your mouth will go dry. In addition, your digestive system will shut down to allow a better supply of blood to the muscles. Your hair will stand on end (piloerection). Your pupils will enlarge so that your vision can improve. Your hand and limbs will also begin to tremble. Once these biochemical mechanisms and processes are fully engaged - and it takes only nanoseconds - your body will be in the fight-or-flight mode.

For most people, the fight-or-flight response has a debilitating effect. They panic or freeze up, and fear then becomes a powerful weapon of the attacker. By paralyzing you with fear, his job is easier.

Survival Weapons

Therefore, it is critically important that you learn to control the fight-or-flight response to make it work for you and not against you in a self-defense situation.

First, accept the fact that the fight-or-flight response is a natural human response. In fact, it's one of Mother Nature's best ways of helping you survive a dangerous situation. You've got to take advantage of this assistance by using the energy of the adrenaline surge to augment your counterattack and awaken your killer instinct. The killer instinct burns on the fuel of adrenaline and can be a vicious and lethal source of energy. Properly channeled, this destructiveness will exceed that of your assailant, and you will overwhelm him.

Second, harness the fight-or-flight response by preparing yourself thoroughly for the danger that may one day confront you. Developing the psychological and physical skills of your self-defense weapon will lead to a personal self-confidence. In turn, this confidence leads to an inner calm. Inner calm is the environment necessary to the killer instinct, and the killer instinct will drink adrenaline like a race horse drinks water.

Your preparation involves learning the physical skills, techniques, and tactics required to use your weapon effectively. The only way to achieve these skills and techniques is with a qualified reality based self-defense instructor and realistic training (e.g., simulated assaults with tough physical contact).

This type of physical training leads to psychological preparedness. Once you begin to understand what a physical confrontation consists of, you can expand your training to visualize such confrontations and the necessary control over the fight-or-flight syndrome.

You must continue to develop this keen sense of self-awareness to be psychologically prepared for a violent confrontation. Never stop assessing your state of mind and reactions to different stressful situations. For example, the next time you are startled by something, pay close attention. What was it that startled you and why? Did you freeze up? What did you see? What did you hear? Were you trembling and breathing heavily? Was your mind clear or distracted? Exactly what were you thinking about? How much detail can you remember? Did you make any tactical errors in your responses? These are only a few of the questions you should answer over and over again as you go through the process of preparing yourself psychologically.

Another method of psychological preparation is written analysis. For example, write down five different hypothetical scenarios (i.e., carjacking, robbery, rape attempt, etc.) that truly frighten you. These scenarios could take place anywhere (home, workplace, street, hiking trail, parking lot). Be specific with your details. Make certain to include the following relevant factors:

- **Time of day**
- **Environment**
- **Attacker's description**
- **Number of attackers**
- **Type of crime**
- **Assailant's intent**
- **Type of physical attack/assault**
- **Type of weapon**
- **Your immediate physical condition at time of attack**
- **Any other relevant factors to your scenario**

Once you've completed these scenarios, have your instructor identify the specific factors that elicit reasonable fear and then adjust your self-defense training to meet your concerns.

In the interim, if you find yourself in a dangerous situation

Survival Weapons

and cannot control your fight-or-flight response and you become overwhelmed with panic, quickly convert your fear into raw, vicious anger. That's right: get mad! Some low-life thug is about to injure or kill you or some loved one. Tear him apart. Relying purely on anger is not the best way of defending yourself, but your raw anger can still be a powerful emotion that can be used in your favor.

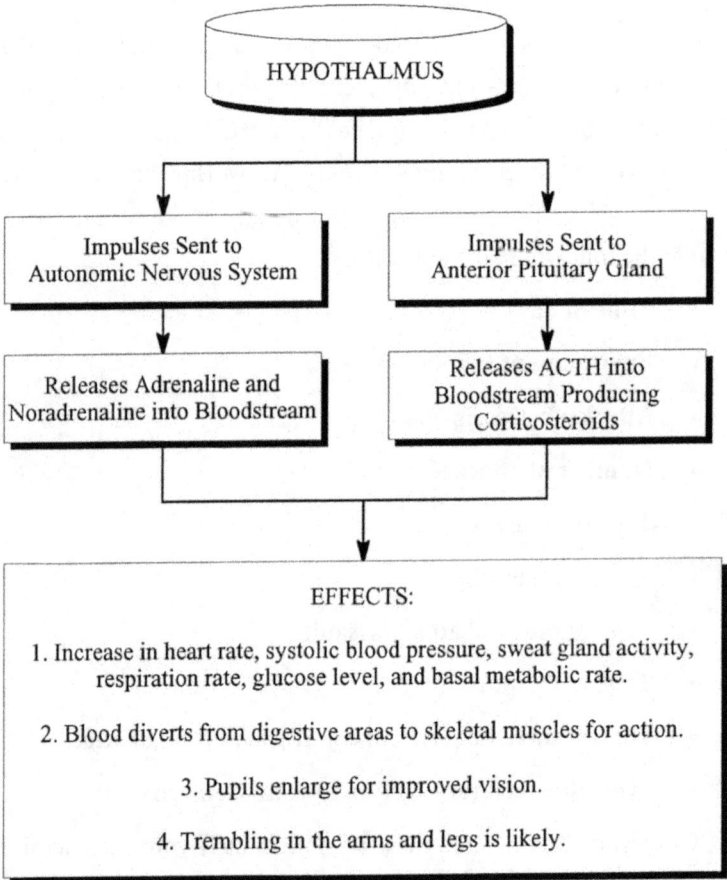

Pictured here, a diagram of the fight-or-flight response.

Possible Physiological Responses To Fear

- Enlarged pupils

- Dry mouth

- Trembling hands

- Cold, clammy hands

- Increased heart rate

- Shutdown of digestive system

- Tense muscles

- Sudden adrenaline surge

- Hair stands on end

- Enhanced alertness

How To Control Your Fear of Violence

Here are a few suggestions that will help you control the deleterious effects of fear:

- Learn the necessary skills and tactics of self-defense.

- Be confident and competent with your weapon skills.

- Regularly practice high-crisis rehearsal (visualization) scenarios.

- Understand and accept the physiological responses to the fight-or-flight response.

- Learn how to tap and control your killer instinct.

- Evaluate your past responses to dangerous or threatening situations.

- Learn the differences between "perceptual danger" and "reasonable danger."

- Always believe in your skills and abilities.

Survival Weapons

- Always trust your instincts and judgments.
- Develop accurate threat assessment skills.
- Adopt the will to survive.
- Always strive to be physically fit.
- Maintain a high degree of situational awareness.
- Regularly practice assault scenarios with a spouse, friend, training partner, etc.
- Always keep a positive mental attitude.

Chapter Two
Survival Weapon Requirements

One Purpose and One Purpose Only!

Let's cut through all the carefully worded and politically correct jargon. Survival weapons are designed to do one thing and one thing only - to injure or kill another living creature. Period! Personal protection weapons can take many different forms and are as varied as the people and institutions that use them.

For example, a seasoned fighter's clenched fist can be a very potent weapon while at the same time so can an ICBM. It has been determined that some of the earliest or ancient weapons (sticks and spears) were created approximately 400,000 years ago for a variety of purposes, including waging war, hunting for food, and personal protection.

Personal protection weapons are used by just about everyone; the military, law enforcement, security specialists, criminals, self-defense practitioners, preppers, survivalists, and well as your everyday

No matter how you slice it, weapons are designed to do one thing and one thing only - to injure or kill another living creature.

layperson. Depending on who's wielding the weapon and for what purpose, it can be used for both good and evil purposes.

Weapons are certainly a controversial subject. They are a hot button topic in politics, religion as well as the local and national media. Some people embraced them while others detest them. Regardless, of your personal opinion, there is no disputing the fact that self-defense weapons are a vital component of human survival and will exist as long as humankind (pardon the pun) occupies this tumultuous planet.

Not All Weapons Are Created Equal!

Self-defense weapons are also a vital component of disaster preparedness, and they play an essential role in any survival situation. For example, a loaded firearm in the hands of a trained homeowner can immediately change the outcome of a home invasion. As you can imagine, there's a wide variety of hand-held weapons available to a law abiding citizen who wants to protect himself or his family from danger and crime. However, not all weapons are created equal for self-defense.

It's important to point out that some weapons are better than others for survival. In fact, a weapons utility is predicated on the specific emergency situation and circumstances you are faced with at that particular moment.

Since every self-defense situation will vary, so will the weapon. For example, if you were attacked in your car, you wouldn't use a grenade to defend yourself. Instead, you would choose a more appropriate tool such as a knife.

Different Strokes For Different Folks

Every person is different and therefore will have different needs. Not every self-defense weapon mentioned in this book is going to suit your requirements. For example, the weapons you might choose for an everyday carry bag might significantly differ from the ones you would carry in a bug out bag. It was the legendary Bruce Lee who stated, *"Absorb what is useful, reject what is useless, add what is specifically your own."* This principle also applies to weapon(s) selection. The bottom line - pick and choose what works for during an emergency or high-risk situation.

Four Survival Weapon Requirements

If a weapon is to be used specifically for self-defense purposes, it must fulfill several essential requirements or the user will be at risk of injury or death. For all intents and purposes, the weapon must be efficient, effective, safe, concealable, and secure. If just one of these criterion is missing, the hand held weapon is not a viable personal protection tool.

- **Weapon Efficiency** - the weapon must be a low-maintenance device that helps its user reach his objective quickly and economically. It must also be immediately accessible and easy to operate under the duress of a high-crisis situation.

- **Weapon Effectiveness** - the weapon must be reliable and produces an immediate desired effect when used.

- **Weapon Safety** - the weapon must provides the least amount of danger and risk for the user.

- **Concealable** - the weapon must be easy to conceal from other people. You don't want to stand out or bring attention to the fact that you might be carrying a weapon on your person or in your survival bag. Remember the gray man theory; you want to blend in with others and ultimately disappear in the crowd during a disaster situation.

- **Secure** - the weapon must be secure from unauthorized individuals gaining access to them when carried on your person or stored in your bag. Luckily, many tactical bags come with cord locking systems that offer a moderate amount of protection from everyday pickpockets.

Nevertheless, the weapons you choose to use and carry will largely depend on your personal preferences, likes, dislikes, comfort zone, skill level, etc. For example, it takes a considerable amount of time setting up a survival bag. You'll need to work with it - experiment and evaluate the items you carry in your bag until you have a smooth system. Remember, your survival bag is going to evolve with time and so will the weapons you choose to carry.

If you choose to carry weapons in your survival bag, you must be certain you can keep them away from thieves.

Weapon Ownership

Finally, weapon ownership is a big decision requiring considerable thought, however if you do decide to own a person protection weapon, it's extremely important that you understand your state and federal laws regarding possession and ownership of various weapons. Moreover, it's also your social responsibility to seek weapons training from a qualified weapons instructor who specializes in reality-based self-defense.

Here are a few important questions you need to ask yourself before you decide to own any self-defense weapon.

1. Exactly why do you want to own a weapon? Give very specific reasons.

2. How do you intend on carrying your survival weapons? For example, are you going to carry them in your car? on your person? in a survival bag? What kind of bag are you going to use (i.e., backpack, sling bag, waist pack, etc.)

3. Are you willing to take the necessary amount of time to acquire the knowledge, skills, and attitude necessary to safely use the weapon?

4. Are you willing to practice with the weapon on a regular basis?

5. Do children or teenagers live in your home? Do they have direct access to your weapons?

6. Will co-workers or strangers have access to your bag and its contents?

7. Do you or any member of your household suffer from alcoholism, drug addiction or depression?

8. Are you a hot-tempered person?

9. Will you be able to safely secure the weapon when it's in your

home, in your car, at work, or on your person?

10. Are you willing to learn the laws regarding the use of your weapon in a self-defense situation?

11. What type of weapon do you want to own? How many?

12. Who else will have access to your car or survival bag?

Concealment is key. Avoid the common tendency to adorn the exterior of your bag with weapons. Remember, you don't want to advertise or bring attention to what you are carrying.

Chapter Three
Get the Lead Out!

Firearms

Without a doubt, the most powerful weapon you can carry is a firearm. Millions of Americans own firearms for a variety of reasons: personal protection, home defense, recreation, hunting, collecting, and competition. Interestingly enough, the number of women owning firearms has increased dramatically to more than 12 million.

Overall, we know that firearm ownership is a controversial issue that has generated tremendous national concern. Some pro gun activists believe that law-abiding citizens have an absolute Constitutional right to bear arms with restrictions. Their opponents, on the other hand, believe that guns are the root of all evil and must be eliminated to address criminal violence in our society effectively.

My opinion on firearm ownership is simple. I think firearms have a very real place in self-defense and personal survival. So long as there are deadly and vicious criminals, there is a need for firearms. Yet I don't believe everyone should own a gun. It's pretty hard to disagree with the position that gun ownership should be restricted to law-abiding citizens who are willing to make the time and commitment to safe, responsible ownership.

The decision to own a firearm for personal protection warrants considerable thought and honest reflection. Here are some important questions to ask yourself:

- Do you abuse alcohol or use drugs?
- Are you hot tempered?
- Could you take the life of another human being?
- Are you subject to long periods of depression?
- Do you live alone?
- Are there children in your household?
- Why do you want a gun?

- Have you ever shot a gun?

- Are you a disorganized person?

- Are you accident prone?

- Are you willing to take the time to obtain the knowledge and learn the skills needed to handle firearms safely?

I hope you get my point. You'd better sit down and have a serious face-to-face talk with yourself before you even visit the gun shop. And remember these scary truths about firearms: many gun owners are killed accidentally by their own weapons, and handguns and shotguns contribute significantly to the death of friends and family members.

Gun ownership carries tremendous social responsibilities. You must be knowledgeable of the circumstances that could justify the use of a firearm in self-defense. However, the laws concerning firearm usage are not something you're going to learn overnight. Using a firearm for self defense is legally complex.

Consider, for example, the scary fact that it is not always justified to use a gun against an intruder in your home. This fact is hard to believe or accept, but it's true. A gun places you in the position of judge, jury, and executioner - all in a matter of seconds.

You are no more qualified to use a gun because you've purchased one than you are to conduct a Beethoven symphony because you own the sheet music. If you are going to own a firearm, learn to use it properly. Get qualified training in safe handling, basic operation and maintenance, and marksmanship. Ideally, children and other family members should be trained as well.

Remember the fallacy of dependency. A gun may not always be there when you need it most, so don't be solely reliant upon one for your or your family's safety. You have to figure out a way to make it readily accessible to you but safely away from the hands of unauthorized people.

The Right Firearm for your Needs

Before you buy a gun, it is your responsibility to understand and obey the various laws governing its use, possession, and transportation. Such laws vary from state to state, so learn the ones that apply to you and your community. Your local police or sheriff's department can tell you.

Purchasing a firearm isn't going to be easy. With so many different guns on the market, it is often difficult to make a choice. However, here are some important questions that will help you with your selection.

- What gun caliber are you considering?
- What is the size and weight of the gun?
- Will you be carrying the gun on your person or in your survival bag?
- What type of survival bag will you use to carry your firearm? Is it designed for CCW?
- How much money are you willing to spend on a particular firearm?

Also consider these helpful tips before buying a gun for personal protection:

- Get advice from firearm experts, survivalists, police officers, and reputable dealers.
- Familiarize yourself with the various models on the market.
- Read various gun/survival magazines and find out which guns have the greatest reliability.
- Read the warranty or guarantee that comes with the firearm.

- Look for high-quality brand-name firearms.

- Know the gun's recoil before you buy it.

- Buy the firearm from a reputable dealer.

- Be certain the firearm fits comfortably in your hand.

- Be certain your gun can be concealed and secure.

- Look for a gun that is easy to clean and operate.

- Be certain the weapon has sufficient "stopping power".

Finally, avoid impulsive purchases because firearms can be very expensive and cannot be returned to the gun shop. If there is a particular gun that interests you, spend some time and do some research on the weapon. Or visit your local gun range and try it out for size. Be patient, it takes time to research a gun purchase.

Pictured here, the concealed carry compartment of Maxpedition's Sitka gearslinger bag.

The 3 Basic Types of Guns

For self-defense purposes, there are three basic types of guns to consider: shotguns, revolvers, and semiautomatics. However, since we are looking exclusively at firearms that can be easily stored, carried or concealed, we are limited to handguns.

Handguns

Some experts argue that handguns are the superior weapon for personal protection. Unlike long guns (shotguns and rifles), handguns (with practice and training) can be transported, drawn, and fired very quickly from your person and your bag. In most armed self-defense survival situations, the handgun is superior to a long gun. Here are just a few reasons why:

1. Unlike rifles and shotguns, handguns can be drawn and fired more quickly with practice and training.

2. Handguns can be transported more easily.

3. Handguns are smaller and can be concealed better on your personal and in your bag.

4. In a close quarter struggle, long guns can be controlled, leveraged and disarmed more easily than handguns.

5. Handguns can, if necessary, be shot with just one hand.

6. Handguns can be holstered, allowing you to utilize other lower "use-of-force" options and tactics on your adversary.

There are two types of handguns I am going to discuss: revolvers and semiautomatics. Let's first take a look at the revolver.

The Revolver

Some people consider the revolver the best type of firearm for personal protection. As you might imagine, it's called a revolver because its cylinder revolves when the trigger is pulled. Revolvers hold anywhere from five to nine cartridges, depending upon the size and capacity of the cylinder. They also come in single action (you have to cock the hammer before it can be fired) or double action (you just squeeze the trigger).

Loading a revolver is safe and straightforward, and you can easily tell when it has rounds in it. They almost never jam, and they can be trusted to fire reliably under some of the most extreme combat conditions.

The operation of a revolver is incredibly simple. Simply squeeze the trigger (assuming it's a double action revolver) or cock the hammer back and it will rotate the cylinder and align a live round of ammunition between the hammer and the barrel of the gun.

The Semiautomatic

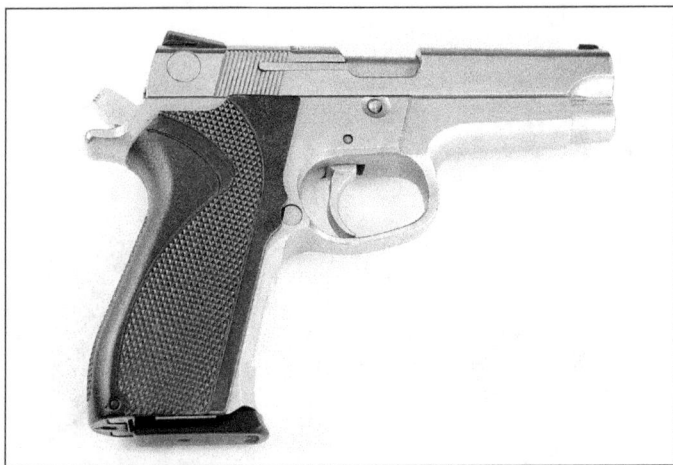

The Semiautomatic pistols differ from revolvers in many ways. They are called "semiautomatics" because when fired they automatically feed a fresh round and eject the spent casing. All you have to do is keep squeezing the trigger. Most full automatics require you to squeeze the trigger once, thus emptying the entire magazine. With the semiautomatic, rounds are loaded vertically in a metal container called the magazine. The magazine is then inserted into the grip of the gun.

One of the main advantages to a semiautomatic pistol is that you can load and reload it very quickly by ejecting the empty magazine and sliding a full magazine back into its place. This type of handgun carries a lot more rounds than a revolver. This is an important consideration when you're confronted by multiple armed attackers. Semiautomatics generally have a lighter trigger pull weight than their revolver cousins, and this can make a difference in accuracy under pressure.

In short, semiautomatics hold more ammunition, can be fired faster, and can be reloaded faster. They are really the ideal weapon for combat, as you might imagine. On the other hand, they are generally more complicated than revolvers. And some experts say they are more dangerous than revolvers because it's harder to know readily if they're loaded.

For personal protection, I prefer the 9mm SIG Sauer P226 combat pistol. It is known for its excellent accuracy, feeding reliability and incapacitation potential. The SIG Sauer P226 has a barrel length of 4.41 inches, weighs approximately 26.5 ounces, and has a magazine capacity of 15 rounds. It has a 12-pound trigger pull on double action and a 4-pound trigger pull on single action.

One of the best features of the SIG Sauer P226 is its moderate recoil. It's no wonder that the SIG Sauer is quickly becoming a favorite weapon among many law enforcement agencies.

Please remember that no matter what kind of gun you buy - if you get one - it isn't going to help you unless you know what you're doing. Get trained by a qualified instructor in firearm personal protection and never forget the fundamental rules of firearm safety.

Pictured here, the Sig Sauer 226 semi automatic handgun with a slide in the rear lock position. This gun is incredibly easy to field strip and clean.

Choosing the Right Gun

One of the most common questions my students ask is, "what is the best handgun for self defense?" Well, in order to answer this question I have to explain the importance of handgun caliber. Essentially, the term "Caliber" refers to the size designations for bullets and the inside diameters of the gun barrels. Also keep in mind that "Caliber" is expressed in units of either inches or millimeters (mm).

For example, a designation like .22, .308, .32, .357, .44, .45, etc refers the approximate outside diameter, in inches, of the bullet and the inside diameter of the barrel. Its also worth mentioning that "gauge" is a term for size designations of shot shells (for shotguns).

.38 Caliber Pistol

The .38 caliber measure thirty-eight hundredths of an inch in diameter. This was a standard round for most law enforcement agencies from 1930's through the 1960's. In fact, the .38 caliber revolvers have been in service since World War II.

Because of its limited round capacity and poor stopping power, the .38 round is not recommended for self defense and personal protection.

9mm Pistol

The 9mm is a popular cartridge was designed to operate in semi automatic and full auto firearms, and is used worldwide by elite military units. The 9mm is the current NATO standard caliber for handgun cartridges.

The 9mm is a great round because of its large shot capacity, low recoil and sufficient stopping power. This cartridge is still one of my personal favorites for self defense. For some of you skeptics who think the 9mm does not have sufficient stopping power - think again. Its merely an issue of using the right cartridge. For example, did you know there is 9mm ammunition that will give you the stopping power of a .45 handgun.

Finally and most importantly, if ever you were faced with a doomsday apocalypse scenario, where ammunition was scarce, the odds of finding 9mm ammunition compared to other calibers will be much greater.

40 Caliber Pistol

The .40 S&W round was essentially designed as a law enforcement cartridge. For some people, the .40 is a middle ground caliber. The .40 round seems to have a bit more muzzle energy than a 9mm and less flash and recoil of a .357 round. This is certainly a good caliber for self defense purposes.

357 Magnum Pistol

The .357 Magnum cartridge was developed by Elmer Keith and Smith & Wesson in 1934. While the .357 Magnum was primarily created for hunting, it was quickly adopted by law enforcement, who needed a round with increased effectiveness against criminals in automobiles. Because of its impressive stopping power, the .357 Magnum is an excellent self defense round. However, keep in mind that this gun will have significant recoil kick back.

.45 Caliber Pistol

This is a "work horse" round that has been around since World War I. The .45 round is well known for its accuracy and stopping power and is considered to be one of the world's more effective self defense handgun cartridges. It has been said that getting shot by a .45 is likened to someone throwing a manhole cover into your chest!

It's no wonder the .45 ACP pistol round is often referred to as a *manstopper*.

.22 Caliber Pistol

When it comes to handguns for self defense, the .22 caliber pistol is not a desirable weapon. While this popular caliber might be great for target practice, it simply doesn't have the stopping power necessary to stop a crazed criminal attacker in his tracks. While it's true that people have died from a .22 caliber gunshot, the round will not reliably stop the immediate threat and in most cases you can get hurt or killed during the altercation.

Reliable stopping power is one of the most important prerequisites of handgun self defense. Essentially, "stopping power" describes a firearms ability to penetrate and immediately incapacitate or "stop" a human target.

Stopping pepper describes a firearms ability to penetrate and immediately incapacitate or stop a human target for continuing deadly aggression.

Holding a Bad Guy at Gunpoint

If you somehow manage to capture and hold the criminal at gunpoint, be sure to keep him at a safe distance and in an awkward position. Make sure that both of his hands are always in clear view. If possible, order him to do the following:

1. Make him turn and face away from you so he can't see what you're doing.

2. Tell him to slowly raise his hands straight over his head. Be certain you can see his fingertips.

3. Have him slowly drop to his knees, without using his hands.

4. Once on his knees, have him cross one leg over the other.

5. Next, have him lie on his stomach with his arms at his sides.

6. Tell him to place his hands flat on the floor with his palms

facing up.

Under no circumstances should you allow him to get within grabbing distance of your firearm. And do not search him for any weapons. Simply keep him in this awkward position until help arrive.

Don't engage in any conversation with him. Bark out your orders firmly and confidently; let him know you mean business. Keep your finger on the trigger and aim the gun at the center of his body. Don't ever take your eyes off him, and be aware that he might have an accomplice close by.

Stay with him until the police arrive, but be careful about greeting the authorities with a gun (or any weapon) in your hand. The first officers on the scene have no way of knowing who is the good guy and who is the criminal. Until they sort things out, keep any weapons out of sight.

Important Firearm Survival Tips

Don't forget - if it's unloaded it's useless - When it comes to personal protection during an emergency situation, never forget that an unloaded firearm is a useless firearm. If you are going to carry a gun in your bag, make sure its loaded and ready to go at all times.

Remember that ability overrides the weapon - Most people don't understand that it is really not the firearm that is important but the skill and ability of the person operating the weapon. Remember, a firearm is only as effective as the person who uses it.

Be on the lookout for concealed weapon carry - Just because you carry a firearm doesn't mean you should be oblivious to others in your environment. Remember, criminals do not usually carry their guns in holsters or survival bags. Train yourself to immediately spot unusual bulges and people who seem to be performing security body pats.

Don't forget, they shoot back - Combat is often very disjointed, hard to understand, and confusing. A gunfight is nothing like what you see on TV or in the movies. It is not romantic or antiseptic. It is horrifying, brutal, confusing, rapid, bloody, and final. And although practice is essential, never forget that training at a firing range has little to do with the explosive dynamics of a lethal gunfight. And, most important, in a real encounter, the targets move and shoot back with cold determination.

Know what you're talking about - Understand the nomenclature of your firearm. The following are some basic terms that you should understand clearly: (1) for the revolver - muzzle, barrel, front and rear sights, ejector rod, cylinder, trigger and trigger guard, frame, grip, cylinder release latch, hammer spur, hammer, firing pin, and chambers; (2) for the autoloader - magazine, cartridge ejection port, slide, grip, frame, front and rear sights, hammer, trigger, trigger guard, recoil spring, slide catch lever, and magazine floorplate.

Rotate spare magazines - Long-term compression of the magazine spring in your semi-automatic can prevent proper cartridge feeding. This is otherwise known as "spring set." Here are two suggestions that will help prevent unnecessary magazine spring stress in your semiautomatic pistol: (1) get into the habit of rotating your spare magazines every three months and (2) don't load your magazine to full capacity; leave at least one or two rounds out.

Remember ammunition criteria - When selecting a self-defense cartridge for your weapon, make certain that your ammunition fulfills these five requirements: (1) stopping power - it must be able to stop your assailant immediately from any further action; (2) controlled recoil - it should allow you to recover quickly from the recoil of your shot; (3) limited ricochet - it should significantly reduce the bullet's ability to ricochet off hard surfaces; (4) maximum penetration - it must be able to go through objects (e.g., car doors, furniture, etc.); (5) reliability - it must be free from various cartridge malfunctions (e.g., hang fire, misfire, or squib loads.)

Master the standing, kneeling, prone, and supine positions - Learn to fire a firearm from a variety of combat positions and stances, including the following: (1) standing position - with or without cover, (2) kneeling position - with or without cover, (3) prone position (lying on your stomach) - with or without cover, and (4) supine position (lying on your back) - with or without cover.

Master combat shooting at various levels - Combat shooting should be practiced from the following four levels: (1) hip level - one- and two- hand grip, (2) chest level - one- and two-hand grip, (3) point shoulder level - one- and two-hand grip, and (4) sighted level (point shoulder level) - two- hand grip.

Never bluff - Finally, never point a firearm at anyone unless you are technically and psychologically prepared to take a life. This also applies to knife combat as well.

Chapter Four
Slash and Thrust

Knives and Edged Weapons

The next survival weapon we are going to address is the knife. Actually, the knife is one of humankind's most ancient weapons, perhaps second only to the club or bludgeon. The earliest knives were scraped and banged out from bone, wood, and even stone and were valuable tools as well as weapons. They played a critical role in conquering game and protecting against threatening invaders. Over the ages, craftsman's skills have been significantly refined.

Today's knives come in many styles and forms and serve many purposes. Thus, they are more readily available to both you and your potential attacker. Therefore, knives are the most commonly used weapons in violent crimes. Incidentally, the knife is the weapon of choice among rapists. Depending on who wields it, the knife can be your best friend - or your worst enemy.

Using a Knife for Self-Defense

The knife is an excellent self-defense weapon. In the hands of the well-trained citizen, a good knife will neutralize or kill any criminal aggressor. Learning to use one, however, requires considerable time and training.

Knives, like guns, or great equalizers. Armed with a knife, a small woman could have a lethal advantage over a 200-pound man. Provided she has proper mental and physical training and a razor-sharp knife, a woman can dispatch a vicious male aggressor in a matter of seconds. Like the firearm, physical strength is no longer a necessary consideration when one is armed with a knife. The truth is, it takes very little power to stab into a vital organ or a major artery.

But don't get me wrong. As with firearms, there is a lot more to knife self-defense than just the knife itself. The best combat knife in the world is no substitute for skill and training. A well-trained combatant can stab and gouge you to death with a pencil. A few essential knife fighting skills are concealment strategies grips and stances, target selection, drawing technique, target awareness, safe handling, footwork, and weapon retention. You can develop these adequately with a qualified reality-based self-defense instructor.

There are hundreds of excellent knives on the market. But you don't need a high-priced survival knife to protect yourself. In many cases, an ordinary butcher knife will more than do the job. Regardless, there are a few important points to keep in mind. For self-defense purposes, the knife should be for slashing as well as stabbing and should fit comfortably in your hand. Avoid all knives with finger grooves; they limit your grip and overall manipulation of the blade.

When it comes to real-world self-defense applications, you don't need a high-priced, survival knife. This is especially true if you frequently carry your survival bag in urban environments.

Size is also an important factor. You must be able to conceal the knife from the public eye at all times. At the same time, it must be sharp and large enough to penetrate the assailant's vital arteries and organs. It should also be light enough for you to manipulate it quickly and easily. I recommend a blade at least four inches with an overall knife weight of approximately eight ounces. I also recommend a lock blade or fixed blade made of high carbon stainless steel. Lock blades stay locked open, preventing an accidental closure on your fingers or hand. Avoid using spring blades, switchblades, stilettos, gravity blades, and folding blades. They are simply too unreliable for self-defense purposes.

Fixed or Folding Blades

There are two types of knives: fixed and folding blades. A fixed blade is a knife that has non-movable parts. A folding blade or folder is a knife that has movable parts which allow you to fold the blade into the handle. For our purposes, I am going to address the folding blade, specifically the tactical folding knife that can be used in a wide range of survival situations and environments.

Pictured here, the Crawford/Kasper Fighting Folder with combo blade. An excellent tactical folder for any self-defense situation.

Tactical Advantages of a Fighting Folder

The tactical folder is an awesome self-defense weapon that can be carried on your person or concealed in your survival bag. In the hands of the well-trained person, a good fighting knife will neutralize any criminal aggressor within seconds. Here are just a few more advantages of a tactical folder for self-defense.

- **Concealable** – Regardless of the size of your survival bag, you can hide a tactical folder reasonably well. This is particularly important for people who use small EDC bags. Remember, getting the most with the least is always the best!

- **Deployment** – When properly set up, you can draw a tactical folder incredibly fast.

- **Psychological Intimidation** - Most people have a primal fear of being cut. A knife gives you a tremendous psychological advantage in a self-defense situation. Just remember never to bluff with a knife - if you pull it out, you better be prepared to use it. Remember, a knife is intended to injure or kill, not intimidate

- **Excellent Close-Quarter Weapon** – A well-trained person can produce devastating results with a tactical folder. In a world saturated with combat technology, the knife remains the ultimate close-quarter combat weapon.

- **It's a Touch Weapon** – Whatever the blade touches, it cuts. Plain and simple!

- **It's a Multi-Directional Weapon** – Unlike a firearm, you can instantaneously change the angle of your attack, if necessary.

- **Knives are Blistering Fast** – A well-trained knife fighter can move his weapon blistering fast. In some cases, too fast for the eyes to see!

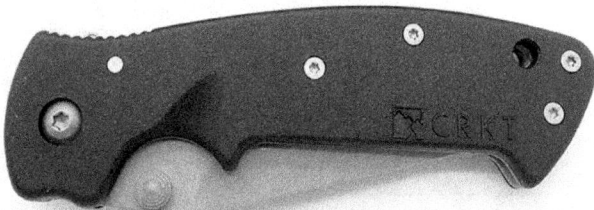

Unlike a fixed blade knife, one of the greatest advantages of a tactical folding knife is the ability to conceal it on your person or in your bag.

- **It's a Great Equalizer** – Against overwhelming deadly force, a knife is a great equalizer. Armed with a knife, a small person could have a lethal advantage over a 250-pound man. Provided the knife wielder has proper mental, physical training, and a razor-sharp knife. Like the firearm, physical strength and power are no longer necessary considerations when one is armed with a knife. The fact of the matter is, it takes little real strength to stab into a vital organ or slash a major artery.

Pictured here, the wrong way to carry a tactical fighting folder. Avoid the tendency to adorn your bag with weapons. You never want to bring attention to the fact that you might be carrying a weapon in your survival bag.

When properly set up, you can draw your tactical folder incredibly fast. Pictured here, a concealed tactical folder and flashlight set up for rapid deployment inside a Maxpedition Sitka gearslinger bag.

There is a lot more to edged weapon self-defense than just the knife itself. The best tactical folder in the world is no substitute for skill and proper training. A few essential skills for knife combat are concealment strategies, grips and stances, target selection, drawing technique, target exploitation, safe handling, footwork, and weapon retention (never drop or lose your knife). You can develop these adequately with a qualified edged weapon instructor. Just remember, learning to use a tactical fighting folder, however, requires considerable time and training.

What to Look For In a Tactical Folder

There are hundreds of tactical folding knives on the market. Some are very good and some are just junk. For self-defense purposes, your tactical folder must be good for slashing as well as stabbing and should fit comfortably in your hand. What follows is a list of important requirements for a good self-defense tactical folder.

Solid Locking Mechanism – You tactical folder must have a solid locking mechanism. Lock blades stay locked open, preventing an accidental closure on your fingers or hand. You want a "linear lock system." It is the safest and most reliable for self-defense applications.

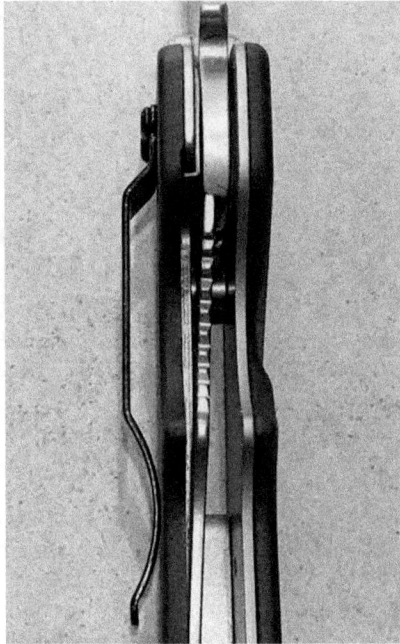

Close-up view of a liner-lock mechanism.

Good Bracing Mechanism – You must be able to hold onto your knife - especially when stabbing with it. Bracing is used primarily with the forefinger. Grooves are used for the thumb area. The handle and digit groove should combine to create an ideal bracing mechanism when you make contact with your target.

Provides Positive Weapon Retention – The ability to retain your knife in the heat of combat is vital. This is especially important when your hands are sweaty or covered with the criminal's blood. Never pick up a knife unless you are confident that you can maintain complete control of it. In my classes I always tell my students, "lose your weapon and you lose your life."

Helps Manage Impact Shock – If your knife hits bone (which is likely) you better have a grip that will manage the impact shock. Remember, cutting the air with your knife is nothing like making hard contact with flesh and bone.

Quick Opening Feature – You want a knife that can open kinetically - meaning it can be opened with the flick of the wrist. I call it a "kinetic opener" because it functions kinetically due to a particular tension where the knife connects. Under stressful conditions, the knife must be opened quickly and positively.

Combo Blade – Your tactical folder must have a partially serrated edge. A serration is simply a sharpened recessed curve along the edge of the blade. Serrations act like teeth that will saw through tough clothing (especially leather). The serrations should also be located on the lower portion of the blade. Caution: Don't use a tactical folder that only has a straight edge, you will regret it! Straight edge blades might not slice through thick fabric like leather jackets.

When looking for a good self-defense knife, always choose one with a partially serrated blade that is capable of slicing through thick material like leather.

Survival Weapons

Sufficient Blade Length - You should be able to conceal the knife from your assailant. However, at the same time, it must be sharp and large enough to penetrate the assailant's vital arteries and organs. I recommend a blade of at least 3.75 inches with an overall knife weight of approximately 7-10 ounces. Remember, that the knife should be light enough for you to manipulate quickly and easily.

Easily Accessible – The folder must be easily and conveniently carried and in a position that is quickly accessible. The best carry system is a clothing clip. Some are made out of plastic or metal and they are either a "point up" or "point down" system. The clothing clip serves two vital purposes. First, it puts the tactical folder in a position that lets you get to it immediately. Secondly, it provides a "predictable orientation" so when you grab your knife (under the stress of combat), you will know exactly how it will be positioned in your hand.

Strong Metal – The blade material of a tactical fighting folder is critical. Cheap knives use 420 steel, so you want at least 440 steel.

Knife Folder Care & Maintenance

Most tactical folders are precision designed and manufactured. Like all precision working tools, they will provide better service and last longer if you follow a few simple Do's and Don'ts, and use the knife in a safe manner.

- Do not use your tactical folder for any task other than cutting. You could damage the knife or yourself, and it will most likely void the manufacturer warranty.

- Do not store your knife in a leather sheath. The leather often collects moisture and creates pits on the blade of the knife.

- Do not use the blade as a can opener, chisel, pry bar, hammer, or screwdriver.

- Do periodically lubricate the blade pivot area with a drop of a WD-40. Although many tactical fighting folders have Teflon bearings, a drop of lubricant will clean the blade pivot area and help the blade open and close more smoothly.

- Do inspect the locking mechanism of the knife regularly to ensure that it will work in a time of need.

- Do keep all dirt, lint, sand and grit out of the knife. Always keep the mechanisms clean.

- Do regularly clean the blade with mild soap and water, and apply a light coat of machine oil with an oil-moistened cloth.

- Do keep the cutting edge sharp. A cutting tool works much better and is safer to use when it is sharp.

- Do periodically check the tightness of the blade pivot screw and other frame fasteners with the appropriate screwdriver, Allen or Torx wrench. Given time and hard use, any blade can loosen slightly.

With respect and a little care, you will get the maximum use from your quality tactical folder. If you have additional questions, do not hesitate to contact the manufacturer of your knife.

Avoid These Types of Knives

- Cheap and poorly made knives
- Knives devoid of a locking mechanism
- Knives with inflammatory words written on them (i.e., killer elite, delta force, punisher, etc.)
- Any images on the knife that denotes violence
- Folder with slippery wooden or metal handles
- All types of spring blades (i.e., switchblades, stilettos)
- Gravity blades

Survival Weapons

- Novelty knives
- Throwing knives

A Word about Throwing Knives

Let me be clear, never throw a knife at your adversary. Frankly, I'm shocked by how many people still think they can pull this off in a self-defense situation. Remember, what works in movies and video games won't work for you in life and death combat encounters. The bottom line is knife throwing will not work under the frightening and spontaneous elements of real-world fighting conditions. Hell, if ever I'm faced with a knife wielding attacker, I hope to God my adversary does throw a knife at me because then I'll have two knives.

Disadvantages of a Knife

Remember what I said about dependency on firearms. The same holds true for knives. Again, the knife is a lethal weapon that can be used only under legally justified circumstances. If you're going to carry a knife in your bag for self-defense, you must assume the legal and social responsibilities that go along with it. Remember, if you are going to use a tactical combat folder in a self-defense situation you had better be absolutely one hundred percent certain your actions are legally and morally justified in the eyes of the law. The use of a knife or edged weapons denotes the use of deadly force and is subject to the laws of each state or local jurisdiction.

Deadly force is defined as violent action known to create a substantial risk of causing death or serious bodily harm. A person may use deadly force in self-defense only if he is protecting himself or a loved one from immediate risk of an unlawful deadly criminal attack. Remember, the decision to use deadly force must always be a last resort; after all other means of avoiding violence has been thoroughly exhausted. You are responsible for you own actions.

Keep in mind, the worst-case scenario in a knife fight is you die; the best-case scenario is you go to prison. Need I say more!

If you're going to buy a knife for self-defense, check your state and local laws. In some states, certain knives are prohibited altogether. Also make certain that if you're going to carry a knife, you do so in a manner consistent with applicable laws.

Finally, a knife is intended to injure or kill, not intimidate. Never pull one out unless you plan to use it. Obviously, knives have a limited scope of application. Since a criminal assailant can take the knife away from you and use it on you, it is imperative that you get adequate training by a qualified instructor.

Chapter Five
Walking Tall

Tactical Cane and Walking Stick

While you can't stuff a tactical cane or walking stick into your survival bag, it's still a fantastic survival weapon that should be added to your personal protection gear.

The purpose of this chapter is twofold. First, it will help you become familiar with the different features of the tactical cane. Second, it will help you choose the right stick for your self-defense needs.

Also, for reasons of simplicity, I'll be using the words "cane" and "walking stick" interchangeably throughout this chapter. Just remember, the self-defense techniques featured in this book can be readily applied with the cane, walking stick, Irish Shillelagh, and even a bo staff.

The walking stick and tactical cane work well with a survival bag set-up.

Why Carry a Cane for Self-Defense?

There are many advantages of using a tactical cane or walking stick for self-defense. First, it is an extremely effective impact tool that allows the average person to administer a devastating blow that far exceeds a typical punch. This fact is especially important for people who are either too small or weak to deliver fisted blows in a fight.

Second, unlike the gun or knife, the cane is ubiquitous tool that can be readily applied during an emergency self-defense situation. A casual stroll through the woods will certainly prove my point.

The walking stick is also versatile. It can be used as an intermediate use-of-force weapon that is useful in a wide variety of fighting environments and circumstances. However, the tactical cane can also be used during extreme self-defense situations, where deadly force is warranted and justified in the eyes of the law.

There are many other reasons why you should consider carrying a cane or walking stick for self-defense, here are a few more:

- It's inconspicuous.
- It's lightweight.
- It's readily available.
- It makes a great everyday carry (EDC) item.
- It doesn't require reloading.
- It won't jam or misfire.
- It's legal to carry.
- It's an excellent impact weapon.

Survival Weapons

- It's both a lethal and non-lethal self-defense weapon.
- It permits a smaller or weaker person to generate tremendous striking power.
- It helps you navigate and climb rocky or unstable terrain.

Regardless of your reasons for carrying a tactical cane or walking stick, remember it's your sole responsibility to research and comply with all local, state and federal laws and regulations pertaining to its possession, carry, and use.

While the walking stick looks inconspicuous, it can also be a very effective self-defense weapon.

Canes and walking sticks are weapons of opportunity that are readily available.

No Two Canes are Alike!

There are hundreds, if not thousands, of different walking sticks on the market, however not all of them are suited for self-defense. In fact, some are downright awful. Choosing the right cane can make all the difference between surviving or dying in a high-risk self-defense altercation.

With so many different types of walking sticks on the market, it can be a bit overwhelming when trying to buy one for personal protection. For example, does it matter if it's made of high impact polypropylene or hardwood? Does it need to have a hook or a knob? Should I buy one that has a sharp point at its end? All of these questions can be answered by first understanding what components make a good tactical cane.

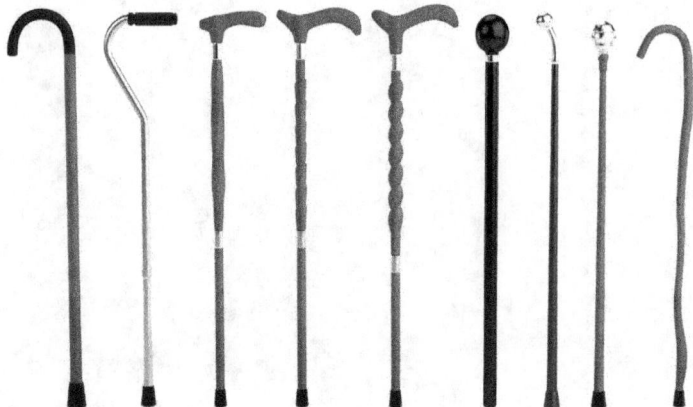

There are thousands of different canes and walking sticks available, however not all of them are designed for self-defense.

What is a Tactical Cane?

So exactly what is a tactical cane or tactical walking stick and why is it so important for personal protection. Essentially, a tactical cane is one that is specifically designed to handle the rigors of an emergency self-defense situation. It should allow you to stop a criminal attacker dead in his tracks through the application of blunt force trauma. To accomplish this task, it must meet the following requirements.

- Sufficient length
- Appreciable weight
- Sufficient thickness

- Structural integrity
- Impact points
- Solid gripping
- Inconspicuous looking

Sufficient Length

For most people, the standard shaft length for a tactical cane is approximately 36 inches. However, you'll find that some walking sticks can be longer in length. In fact, some are as long as a bo staff. For our purposes, just be sure your cane or walking stick has a minimum length of 36 inches.

Appreciable Weight

If you intend on using your cane as a striking weapon, then it must have a minimum weight of approximately twenty ounces. Stick weight is important for one simple reason - striking power! Remember, your cane must have the capability to inflict immediate injury to your attacker.

Unfortunately, some commercial canes are made of lightweight aluminum, making them useless as self-defense weapons. Remember, you must have weight behind your cane strike. It must be hefty enough to incapacitate a large and powerful criminal attacker.

Sufficient Thickness

The shaft of your cane must also have a bit of thickness to it. Again, since its going to function as an impact weapon, it must it have a minimum circumference of 4.5 inches.

Structural Integrity

A tactical cane must be made of durable material that can withstand high impact. Avoid using canes that are made of hollow aluminum or light wood. Instead, find one that is constructed of either high impact polypropylene or hardwood.

Impact Points

Be sure your cane has impact points or ridges running down the shaft of the stick. This is important because it helps concentrate the force of your strike at the point of contact. A good example is Cold Steels Irish Blackthorn Shillelagh walking stick (figure right) which has clipped thorns on the shaft for both concentrated impact and weapon retention.

Solid Gripping

A tactical cane must have a solid gripping surface. Avoid using canes or walking sticks that have smooth polished shafts or high-gloss finishes, because they can become very slippery when your hands get wet from sweat, water, or blood.

Inconspicuous Looking

A tactical cane should also look harmless to the layperson. Remember, the last thing you want to do is bring attention to your weapon. Avoid carrying a cane that looks dangerous or threatening to other people. Avoid carrying one that have skulls, spikes, blades, sharp points, or any designs that look menacing.

What About The Hook?

Despite what some people might say, you don't need a hook on your cane for it to be effective for personal defense. In fact, the hook portion of the cane is more of a novelty than anything else. Worst of all, it can be a big liability during a self-defense situation. Let me explain.

One of the most important concerns when using a cane for self-defense is weapon retention. In other words, it's essential for you to maintain control of your weapon at all times. Remember, if you attacker gets hold of your cane for even a second, it could be lights out for you.

Hooking, trapping or pinning your opponent's arms, groin, or legs with the hook of the cane can often result in a struggle with him. Moreover, attempting to leverage your opponent's limbs with your cane will likely result in him grabbing hold of your weapon and wrestling it away from you. This is especially true for smaller and weaker people who don't have the physical strength or endurance to engage in a tug of war match with their attacker. Fortunately, you can still use a hooked wooden cane for self-defense, just don't use the hook to ensnare your adversary.

The true combat utility of any tactical cane is to stop your attacker dead in his tracks through the application of blunt force trauma to specific vulnerable targets. It's that plain and simple!

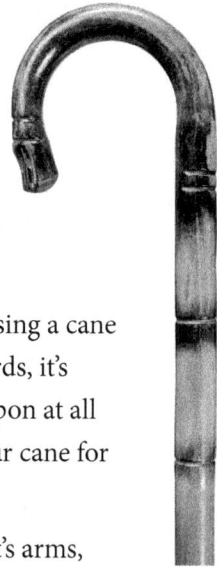

Wooden Cane Nomenclature

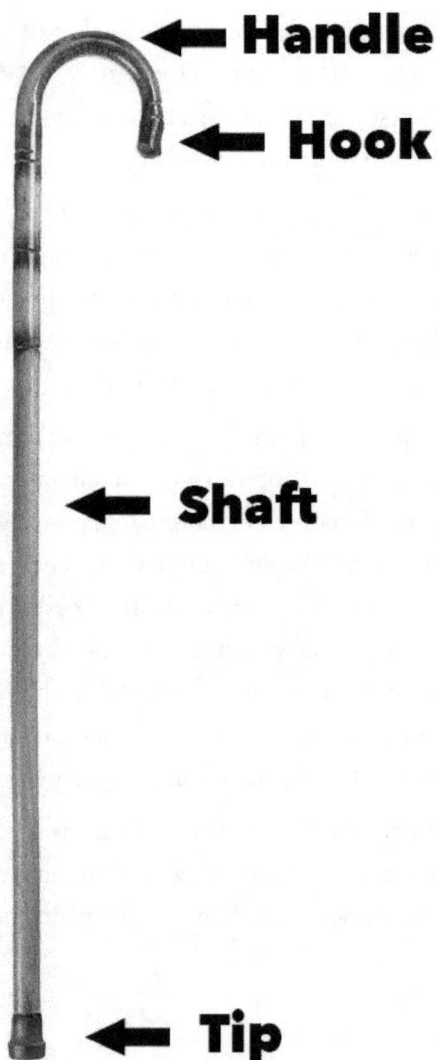

← **Handle**

← **Hook**

← **Shaft**

← **Tip**

Tactical Cane Nomenclature

← **Handle**

← **Impact Ridges**

← **Shaft**

← **Secure Gripping**

← **Tip**

The Irish Shillelagh

The truth is some of the best combat canes and walking sticks don't even have a hook. Take, for example, the Irish Shillelagh or blackthorn stick that is most often associated with Irish stick fighting.

This stout black stick has a large knob at the top that can easily cleave bone and split open a human skull. In fact, some Shillelaghs have their knobs hollowed out and then filled with molten lead to increase the striking force of the stick.

Shillelaghs are usually made from knotty blackthorn wood or oak because they are dense and heavy and less likely to crack during combat. Please believe me when I say that you never want to be at the wrong end of this stick!

The Irish club or Shillelagh is both a wicked fighting tool and stylish walking stick, capable of inflicting tremendous damage. Pictured top, a traditional Irish Shillelagh. Pictured bottom, Cold Steel's modern interpretation of the Irish Blackthorn Shillelagh. Both are considered excellent tactical walking sticks.

Chapter Six
Too Hot to Handle

The Truth About Self-Defense Sprays

Self-defense spray is one of the cheapest personal protection items you can add to your survival bag. There are three types of sprays currently on the market: CN, CS, and OC. However, not all of the spray irritants are effective for self-defense. Let's take a look at each one.

CN or Mace

CN, or Mace, is a chemical tear gas. When sprayed in the attackers face, it causes tearing, burning of the eyes, and minor difficulty in breathing. While CN may sound effective, I don't recommend it for self-defense. First, Mace won't work on crazed assailants who have a high tolerance to pain; such as psychotics, drug abusers, and violent drunks. In most cases, Mace will only make them angrier and more violent. CN can also take up to five seconds to work on the attacker - which is a relatively long time when fighting for your life. Since animals don't have any tear ducts, Mace is also ineffective against vicious dogs.

CS Gas

CS was first used by the US military in 1960. CS is similar to CN, but it is much more potent. When sprayed in the attackers face, it causes tearing, extreme burning of the eyes and skin, coughing, and tightening of the chest. Like its Mace cousin, CS should not be used for self-defense. It simply takes too long to work on the assailant (approximately 30 seconds).

Oleoresin Capsicum (aka Pepper Spray)

Oleoresin capsicum (also known as OC) is a natural mixture of oil and cayenne pepper. Oleoresin capsicum is found in OC self-defense spray or "pepper spray" and it's an inflammatory agent that affects the assailant's mucus membranes (i.e., eyes, nose, throat, and lungs). When oleoresin capsicum is applied to the mucus membranes, the following reactions will occur:

- Eyes will tear and swell shut
- Impaired motor skill function
- Impaired muscle coordination
- Severe burning sensation
- Impaired vision for approximately ten minutes
- Restricted breathing for about thirty minutes

Oleoresin capsicum self-defense spray is sold in a variety of different concentrations (anywhere from five to ten percent). However, these percentages can often be confusing and misleading because the effectiveness of OC is determined by its strength and not its percent of volume. Essentially, OC strength depends on the grind of the pepper before the oil is extracted.

OC is, by far, the best spray for self-defense because it is potent and works almost immediately on the assailant. Unlike mace or CS, pepper spray will incapacitate your attacker regardless of his tolerance to pain. When used properly, OC spray can stop psychotics, drug users, angry drunks, and even vicious animals. Depending on the model you purchase, spray distances will vary from 8 to 10 feet. Believe it or not, some brands will even shoot up to 40 feet.

95

Unlike Mace and CS gas, oleoresin capsicum is the best self-defense spray available.

More Physical Effects of Oleoresin Capsicum

Skin Exposure

- Blistering
- Redness
- Swelling
- Intense burning sensation

Respiratory Exposure

- Inability to speak
- Gagging
- Gasping for air
- Shortness of breath
- Wheezing
- Intense burning of the throat

Nasal Exposure

- Intense headache

- Sneezing

- Reflex mucus secretion

If you intend to carry or use pepper spray for self-defense, get training from a qualified self-defense instructor. You must learn several important tactics before using this weapon for personal protection.

A word of caution: before you purchase or carry pepper spray, check your local and state laws regarding its possession and use. For more information, contact your local police or sheriff's department.

The Limitations of Self-Defense Sprays

Like all hand-held weapons discussed in this book, self-defense sprays have their limitations. First, you must always have the unit in your hand and ready to fire when attacked. Remember, it won't do you any good if the canister is at the bottom of your bag when you are suddenly jumped by an attacker. The conditions of your environment also play a critical role. For example, if you are outdoors and there is a strong wind, the spray should not be used.

Aerosol canisters have also been known to clog and jam. Also, you cannot spray someone in a confined area like a car, bathroom stall, or small closet. Keep in mind that if the assailant holds his breath and closes his eyes, the spray won't stop him from attacking and injuring you. Above all, do not make the mistake of dependency. Remember that no single weapon will guarantee the safety of you and your family.

Scorching

Scorching is a unique and unorthodox use of oleoresin capsicum that is discussed in my book, Feral Fighting: Advanced Widow Maker Fighting Techniques. Scorching is the process of inconspicuously applying oleoresin capsicum to your fingers tips and then raking the opponent's eyes and other mucus membranes.

Scorching is a devastating self-defense tactic that is, by far, the most excruciating form of hand-to-hand combat. It's particularly useful for people who frequent dangerous, high-risk environments and who want to amplify their self-defense skills.

As I stated earlier, oleoresin capsicum is a natural mixture of oil and cayenne pepper. It's an inflammatory agent that affects the assailant's mucus membranes (i.e., eyes, nose, throat, and lungs). When oleoresin capsicum (liquid form) is applied directly to the mucus membranes with your finger tips, the following reactions will occur:

- Eyes will tear and swell shut,
- Impaired motor skill function
- Impaired muscle coordination
- Severe burning sensation
- Impaired vision for approximately ten minutes
- Restricted breathing for about thirty minutes

Warning! Do not use an aerosol pepper spray canister to apply oleoresin capsicum to your fingertips. This is hazardous because you will most likely contaminate yourself and it significantly reduces the potency of OC. Effective scorching will require you to find oleoresin capsicum in a liquid form that can be directly applied to your fingers. There are several on-line manufacturers that sell oleoresin capsicum in liquid form.

Pictured here, Sammy Franco holding a bottle of oleoresin capsicum in liquid form.

There are a couple of ways of applying liquid oleoresin capsicum to your fingertips. One of the best methods is to use my ink pad method, which is inexpensive and just requires you to purchase a dry ink pad from a local office supply store.

Simply pour a liberal amount of liquid OC on the dry pad. To prevent the oleoresin capsicum from evaporating, keep the lid closed at all times and only open it when you must apply it to your fingertips. It's also a good idea to regularly check the ink pad to see if OC residue still remains on the pad.

A word of caution! It's your responsibility to check with your local police department regarding the possession and transportation of liquid oleoresin capsicum.

The ink pad method of application is inexpensive and just requires you to purchase a dry ink pad from any office supply store.

Just like a self-defense spray canister, the OC ink pad can easily be transported in your survival bag. Here, the author demonstrates the ink pad method of application.

Over the years, I've conducted hundreds of simulated test scenarios with my students and have determined that you can load liquid oleoresin capsicum on your fingers in less than three seconds. These tests were conducted using my ink pad method of carry. However, a three-second load time requires proper training and practice, and much will also depend on how you carry your liquid OC.

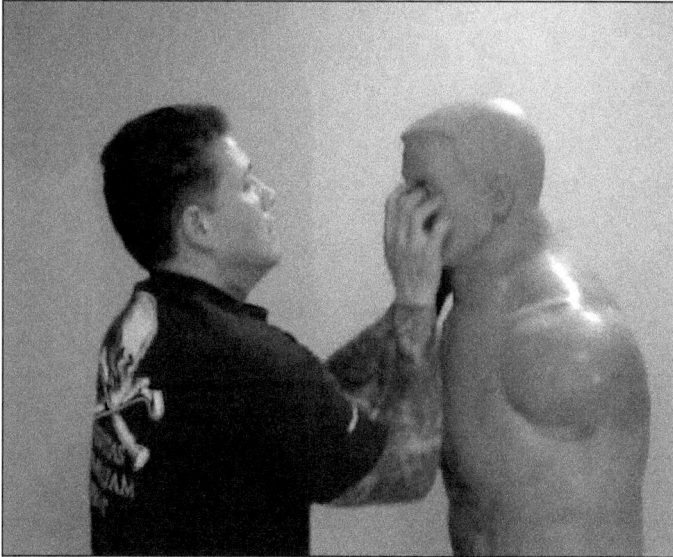

Pictured here, Sammy Franco practices scorching techniques on the body opponent bag.

Just like carrying a concealed firearm, tactical folder, kubotan, or pepper spray canister, scorching requires you to anticipate danger so you can "prepare and load" the liquid oleoresin capsicum on your fingers before the altercation takes place.

Obviously, if you are ambushed or attacked by surprise, you won't have the time apply the OC and therefore won't be able to scorch you adversary.

When setting up for your scorching attack, remember to keep

Survival Weapons

both of your hands up and away from your face. Once the opponent has lowered his guard, and you're in striking range, attack him with a lightning quick finger jab or eye rake.

Chapter Seven
The Mini is the Mighty

What is a Kubotan?

The Kubotan is a close-quarter self-defense weapon that can be used as both an impact tool and pain compliance device. This sturdy mini stick is approximately the size of a thick magic marker and it often has a keyring attached to its end.

The kubotan can be made out of a wide range of different materials, including steel, aluminum, wood and unbreakable plastic. However, the most destructive types are made of solid steel.

Unlike other self-defense weapons, the kubotan is discreet and looks innocuous. The average people will view it as nothing more than a nondescript keychain and therefore can be transported and concealed very easily. Best of all, the kubotan is inexpensive and can be easily purchased.

Why Carry a Kubotan?

There are a number of reasons you should carry a kubotan on your person or in your survival bag. First, a kubotan functions as a highly effective impact tool. It permits the average person to effectively defend themselves by delivering devastating blows that far exceed a typical punch. This is particularly important to people who are too small or weak to deliver fisted blows.

With proper training, the kubotan can also function as both a pain compliance and leverage tool when applying joint locks or submission holds.

From a use-of-force perspective, the kubotan is versatile.

Unlike a firearm and knife, the kubotan can be used as an effective intermediate use of force weapon that can be applied in a wide variety of fighting environments. However, it can also be used during the most dire self-defense circumstances where lethal force is warrant and justify in the eyes of the law.

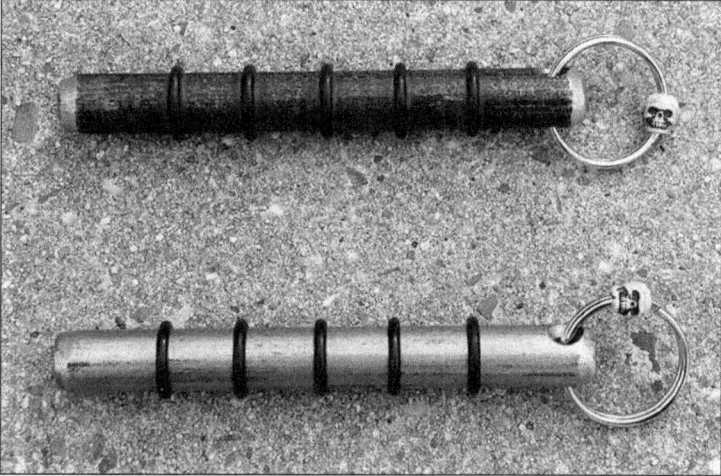

Pictured here, custom made steel kubotans from the author's personal collection.

There are many other reasons why you should consider carrying a kubotan for self-defense, here are a few more:

- It's lightweight.
- It's inconspicuous.
- It's small and can be carried in just about any EDC bag.
- It doesn't require reloading.
- It won't jam or misfire.
- It can be used as a pain compliance tool.
- It can be used as an impact weapon.
- It can be used as both a lethal and non lethal weapon.

- It permits smaller or weaker people to generate tremendous striking power.

- Kubotan techniques can be applied to other survival items such as mini flashlights, tactical pens, yawara palm sticks, etc.

Important: Regardless of your reasons for carrying a kubotan, remember it's your sole responsibility to research and comply with all local, state and federal laws and regulations pertaining to the possession, carry, and use of a kubotan.

Your kubotan should be readily available. However, unless you are specifically using it as a keychain, avoid hanging it from the exterior of your bag.

Choosing The Right Kubotan

There are a wide variety of kubotans on the market, some are good and downright horrible. For example, the spiked kubotan is popular and sold by the thousands, however it's still a very poor choice for real world self-defense applications.

First, the spikes restrict your ability to use certain hand grips. Essentially, the spiked kubotan will only permit you to use the "center point grip."

Second, if you decide to deliver a punch (called fist loading) with this type of kubotan, the spikes will significantly reduce the power of your strike. In the best case scenario, you end up poking two small holes in the attacker's face, causing him to be further enraged.

Third, the spikes turn the kubotan's innocuous and nondescript characteristics into a menacing looking weapon. From a legal perspective, this can be problematic for you. Imagine having to explain why you were carrying such a "dangerous looking" weapon to a police officer, judge or jury.

Although some people prefer the spiked kubotan, it's not recommended for real world survival applications.

With so many different types of kubotans on the market, it can be a bit overwhelming when trying to buy one. Does it matter if it's made of plastic or metal? Does it need to have a keyring attached to it? Should I buy one that has a sharp point at its end? What is the ideal kubotan for self-defense?

What follows, is a list of important characteristics you should keep in mind when buying a kubotan for your survival bag.

Weight Requirement

For a kubotan to be an effective survival weapon, it must have a bit of weight. For all intent and purposes, it should have a minimum weight of approximately seven ounces. This weight is important for one simple reason - impact power!

When a kubotan has this amount of appreciable weight, it will magnify the impact of the actual strike. This is especially important if you are going to use "fist loading" techniques. I'll discuss fist loading techniques later in this book.

The unfortunate fact is most commercial kubotans are made of lightweight aluminum that weighs approximately two or three ounces. Most people like this lightweight feature because it makes the kubotan less cumbersome, especially when it's used as an everyday carry item.

However, this lightweight feature is not ideal for self-defense purposes. The bottom line is, you need the extra weight if you want the kubotan to be an effective self-defense weapon.

Frankly, it all boils down to priorities. If you are using a kubotan as a simple keychain, then it doesn't really matter how much it weighs. Just attach your keys to it and you are done!

However, if you are carrying a kubotan for self-defense purposes, then you owe it to yourself to carry one that is hefty enough to effectively incapacitate a vicious criminal attacker. So, make certain it weighs a minimum of seven ounces.

Length Requirement

The next requirement is length. Make certain your kubotan has a minimum length of 5.5 inches. This should not be much of a problem considering most commercial kubotans will almost always measure approximately 5.5 inches long. This length requirement is important to accommodate large hands and for implementing leveraging techniques.

Keyring Attachment

The keyring attachment is important for two reasons. First, it converts this self-defense weapon into a practical keychain allowing you to carry it on your person or on your bag at all times. Second, it makes the kubotan look less threatening to others. Remember, your kubotan should appear innocuous. This is especially important if your self-defense situation eventually turns into a legal battle.

Believe it or not, the keyring is an important component of the kubotan.

Dark or Muted Color

Purchase a kubotan that is dark or muted in color. Black is preferred. This is important when defending against an attacker in dark or low light conditions.

Avoid using a bright or shiny kubotan. For example, you don't want light to shine off your kubotan when attempting to conceal it from your adversary.

Innocuous Looking

As I stated earlier, a kubotan should look harmless to the layperson. The last thing you want to do is bring attention to your weapon. Avoid carrying a kubotan that has spikes, sharp points or any type of designs that look threatening or menacing.

Also, just because a kubotan doesn't look menacing doesn't guarantee that you won't be stopped by the police. As a matter of fact, the TSA classifies the kubotan as a "martial arts & self-defense item" and prohibits it as a carry on item. So, remember to check it in when flying.

Avoid carrying a kubotan that looks dangerous or threatening. Pictured here, a pointed kubotan that looks menacing, if not sinister.

Flat Ends

The kubotan should have a two flat ends. Avoid carrying one with a pointed tip. Remember, the kubotan is an "impact weapon" and pain compliance tool, not a cutting or puncturing device.

When used correctly, the kubotan it designed to break bones and damage soft tissue. Puncturing the assailant's skin with a pointed tip will certinly not incapacitate a well seasoned criminal attacker.

Kubotan Nomenclature

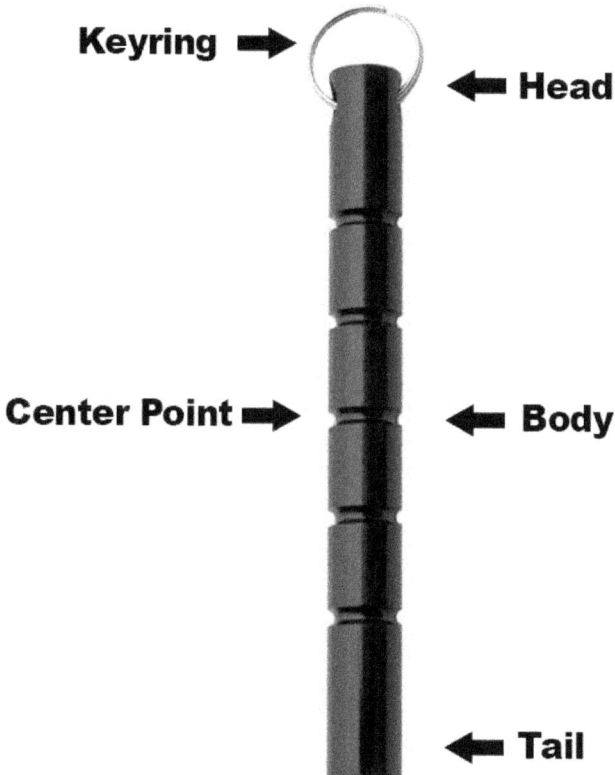

Like any survival weapon, take the time to become familiar with the kubotan's nomenclature.

Chapter Eight
Let There be Light!

Tactical Flashlights

There might be circumstances that prohibit you from owning or carrying a kubotan in your bag. In such a situation, you can replace it with other ubiquitous items, such as a tactical flashlight. Just be certain that the item you choose meets the same requirements discussed in the previous chapter.

Believe it or not, the tactical flashlight is a great alternative to the kubotan. And in some cases, is superior to the kubotan. That's right! It's better. Let me explain why.

First, the tactical flashlight is an illumination tool that allows you to see in the dark or during low light conditions. Second, a good tactical flashlight can temporarily blind and disorient your attacker, allowing you to either strike or escape to safety. Third, you can perform the very same techniques with a tactical flashlight that you can with a kubotan.

Finally, the tactical flashlight is one of the most discreet looking weapons on the planet, making it less menacing looking than any kubotan or fist loading tool on the market.

Choosing a tactical flashlight to replace a kubotan will boil down to personal preference. However, here are a few requirements to keep in mind when choosing one specifically for self-defense applications.

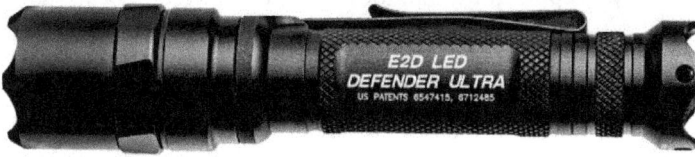

The SureFire E2D LED Defender Ultra Flashlight.

Tactical Flashlight Requirements

If you are considering replacing a kubotan with a tactical flashlight, be certain it meets some of the following requirements:

- The more powerful the bulb the better, just be certain it's impact resistant.

- The flashlight's construction must be solid, allowing you to use it effectively as an impact weapon.

- The ergonomics of the flashlight should permit you to hold it comfortably using any type of kubotan grip.

- The flashlight's construction and materials should provide a sturdy grip to help minimize impact shock.

- When held in its center, the flashlight should protrude at least 3/4 of an inch on each end of your fist.

- The flashlight should weigh a minimum of seven ounces.

- It should be dark or muted in color.

- It should have a clip or carrier system that permits instant access and rapid deployment from either your bag or your person.

- It should have a pushbutton tail cap.

- It should come from a reputable company, known for its quality and reliability.

Survival Weapons

Finally, keep in mind that location is everything. Location, location, location. A tactical flashlight is useless if it is buried in the bottom of your survival bag or left in your car. With a bit of research you can find a flashlight pouch that will easily attach you your bag.

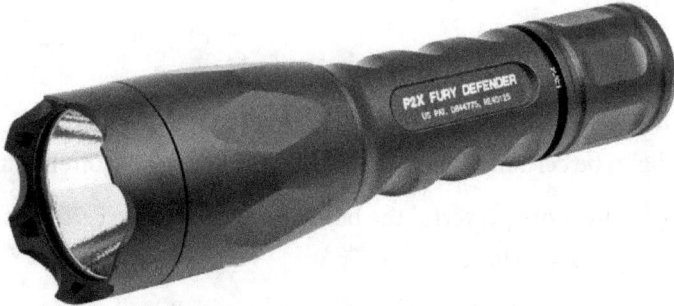

Surefire makes some of the best illumination tools in the world. Pictured here, the P2X Fury Defender.

Nitecore MT21A tactical flashlight.

Nitecore MH2c tactical flashlight.

Fenix LD22 tactical flashlight.

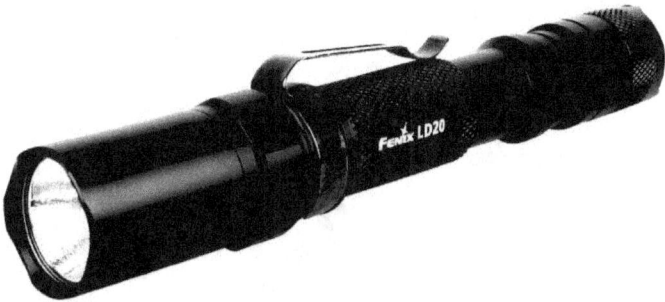

Fenix LD20 tactical flashlight.

When properly set up, you can draw your tactical flashlight incredibly fast. Pictured here, a concealed flashlight set up for rapid deployment.

117

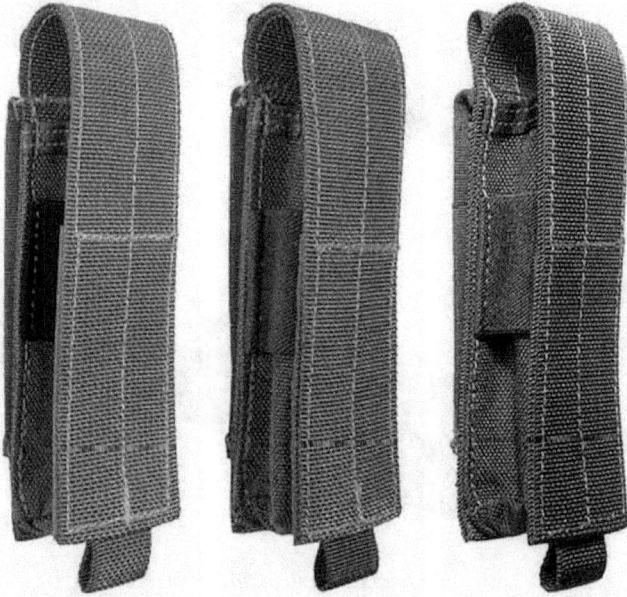

There are some great flashlight pouches on the market. Pictured here, Maxpedition's five inch Flashlight Sheath will attach to just about any bag out there.

Chapter Nine
Mightier Than the Sword?

The Tactical Pen

Some folks make the common mistake of assuming the tactical pen or *self-defense pen* is a suitable replacement for the kubotan or tactical flashlight. It's not. Actually, I strongly encourage you to use a kubotan or a tactical flashlight over a tactical pen. Let me explain.

The main problem with using a tactical pen as an impact weapon is its sharp impact point. This means the pen functions as a puncturing tool that delivers shallow puncture wounds instead of blunt force trauma. While a puncturing tool can be effective under certain self-defense conditions, it's still limited in scope and application. Its biggest drawback as a puncturing tool is its intended target(s).

However, this doesn't mean the tactical pen isn't a viable survival weapon. It's still a good backup weapon if you don't have anything else available. I personally recommend the Hoffman Richter Stinger Tactical Pen. Not only is it durable and discreet, it comes with a Lifetime Warranty.

In order for a tactical pen to be effective, it must make contact with relatively soft and fleshy targets like the eyes and throat. The three best targets for a tactical pen are the eyes, throat and hands. Let's take a closer look at each one.

Eyes

The eyes are ideal targets for a tactical pen attack because they are extremely sensitive and difficult to protect. The eyes can be poked, raked, and gouged from a variety of angles and vantages. Depending on the force of your strike, it can cause numerous injuries, including watering of the eyes, hemorrhaging, blurred vision, temporary or permanent blindness, severe pain, rupture, shock, and even unconsciousness.

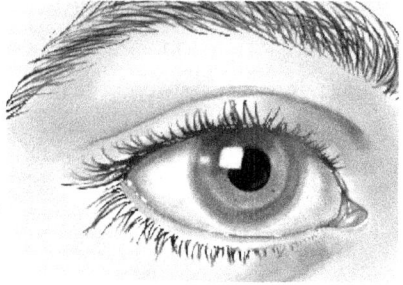

Throat

The throat is considered a lethal target because it is only protected by a thin layer of skin. This region consists of the thyroid, hyaline, cricoid cartilage, trachea, and larynx. The trachea, or windpipe, is a cartilaginous cylindrical tube that measure four and a half inches in length and approximately one inch in diameter. A direct and powerful strike to this target may result in blood drowning, massive hemorrhaging, strangulation, and death. If the thyroid cartilage is crushed, hemorrhaging will occur, the windpipe will quickly swell shut, and the assailant will die of suffocation.

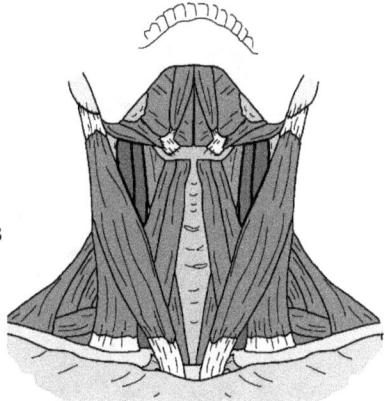

Hands

The fingers and hands are exceptionally weak and vulnerable and make ideal striking targets. The fingers can easily be jammed, sprained, broken, and torn. While a broken hand might not stop a determined fighter, it will certainly force him to release his hold.

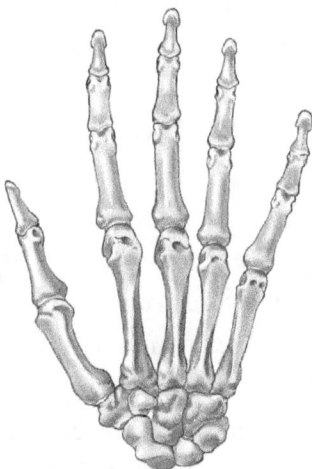

Pictured bottom right, a Hoffman Richter Stinger Tactical Pen hidden inconspicuously on the exterior of a Get Home Bag.

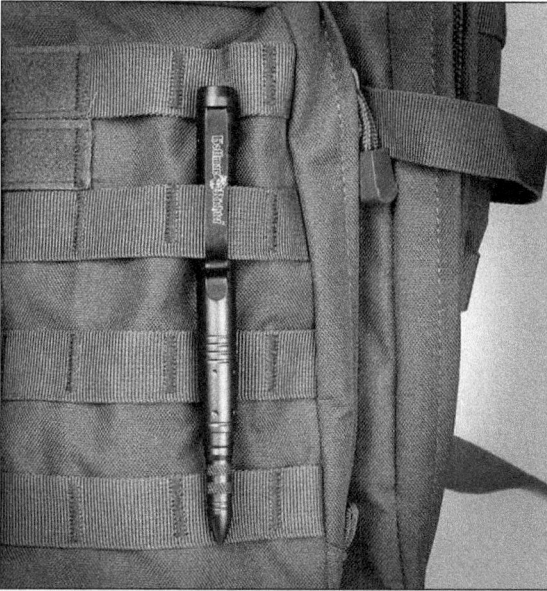

As I've stated throughout the book, keep all survival weapons hidden and secured on your person or in your bag. Don't make this mistake. Remember, if a criminal has quick access to your weapon, he can use it on you.

Holding a tactical pen correctly is essential during a self-defense situation. Pictured here, the modified icepick grip used for powerful stabbing action.

123

Chapter Ten
A Fistful of Pain

Fist Loading Tools

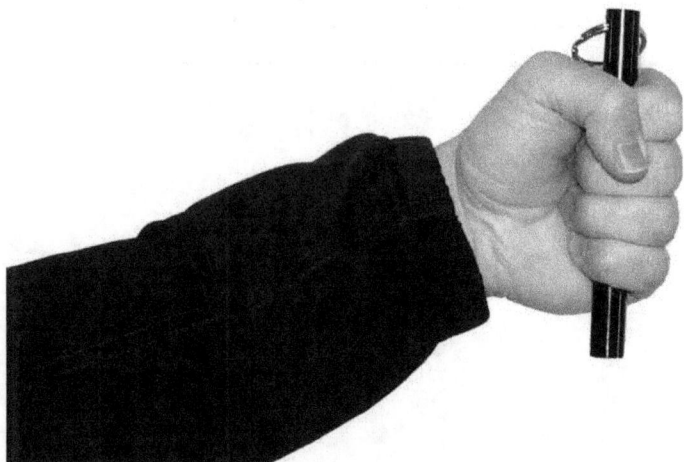

Fist loading is the process of delivering fisted blows with a weighted object concealed in your hand. The added weight of the item in your hand can significantly increases the power of a conventional punch. However, the fist loading object must meet two important requirements:

- **Weight** - If you want to pack a wallop, the object must have a minimum weight of seven ounces. It's this slight, extra weight that amplifies the power of your blow.

- **Structural Integrity** - The object must be solid in construction and provide the structural integrity to reinforce your fist and prevent it from collapsing during impact with its intended target.

Some practical and effective fist loading objects include the following items:

- Metal kubotans

- Yawaras

- Tactical flashlights

- Rolled coins (quarters or nickels are preferred)
- Cylindrical piece of metal
- Long spark plug socket

Once again, if you are going to use a kubotan as a fist loading weapon, it must have a minimum weight of seven ounces. This is why I instruct my students to use steel kubotans instead of aluminum. Believe me, the extra few ounces are worth its weight in gold!

Finally, I'd be remiss if I didn't mention that brass knuckles are one of the best fist loading tools known to man. Unfortunately, they are illegal, and therefore, should not be used in a fight.

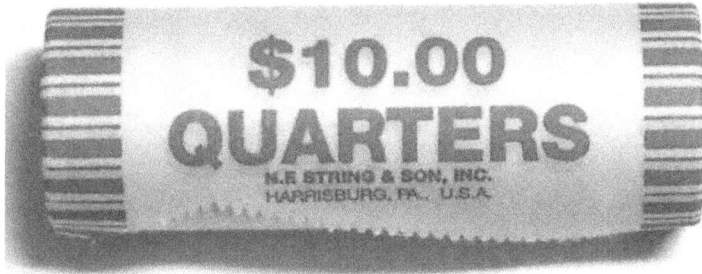

As simple as it may seem, a roll of quarters makes a great fist loading weapon.

Injury Free Punching

Since fist loading requires you to hit with your fists, it's essential that you know how to punch without sustaining a hand injury. Essentially, this requires you to understand and ultimately master a few concepts and principles. Keep in mind, you do not have to be a professional fighter or martial arts expert to master these fundamental principles.

Brass knuckles (also known as knuckle dusters) are the best fist loading weapon known to man. Unfortunately, they are illegal.

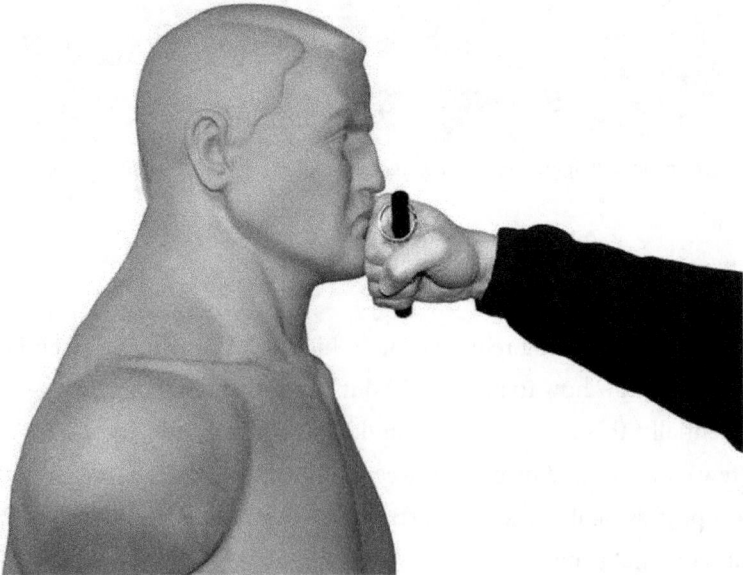

Fist loading techniques should be practiced on a regular basis. In this photo, the author demonstrates a conventional fist loaded punch on the body opponent bag.

What Causes Hand Injuries?

There are four primary causes of punching related hand injuries. They are: incorrect fist configuration, skeletal misalignment, weak hands, wrist and forearms and hitting the wrong anatomical target.

Moreover, while there are different body mechanics for each and every punch, there are four things that must take place to avoid a hand injury, when hitting an assailant. They include the following:

- Knowing how to make a proper fist
- Possessing strong hands, wrists, and forearms
- Maintaining skeletal alignment when striking
- Pinpoint target accuracy
- How to Make a Proper Fist

The first thing you'll need to learn is how to make a proper fist. It's ironic that some of the most experienced fighters don't know how to make a combat ready fist. As you can imagine, improper fist clenching can be disastrous for some of the following reasons:

- You can jam, sprain, or break your fingers
- You can destroy wrist alignment, resulting in a sprained or broken wrist.
- You'll lose significant impact power when hitting your adversary

To make a proper fist, make sure your fingers are tightly clenched and that your thumb is securely wrapped around your second and third knuckles. Your fist should resemble a solid brick. Remember, if you cannot make a proper fist, you will not be capable of delivering a solid fist loading blow.

By the way, long fingernails will compromise the structural integrity of your punch by causing your fingers to protrude from your fist. This can easily lead to a debilitating hand or wrist injury. If you are serious about using a fist loading weapon, consider keeping all of your fingernails short.

Pictured here, the correct way to make a fist.

You Must Keep Everything Straight

Now that you know how to make a proper fist, your next step is learning how to maintaining skeletal alignment when your fist makes contact with the target. Skeletal alignment will help ensure that both your hand and wrists will not buckle and break during impact with the opponent's target.

One of the biggest mistakes people make when making a fist is allowing their thumbs to protrude outward. This hand position is dangerous and can often lead to hand and finger injuries as well as powerless blows. Remember, always to keep your thumbs tightly wrapped around the other two fingers when throwing punches.

Center Knuckle Contact

In order to maintain skeletal alignment when punching, you

need to learn to hit with your center knuckle first. Punching with the center of your knuckle is important because it affords proper alignment and maximizes the impact of your blow.

Excluding hammer fist strikes, every conceivable punch (i.e., lead straight, rear cross, hook, uppercut, shovel hook, etc.) can be delivered with center knuckle contact.

Center knuckle contact also prevents a broken hand or boxer's fracture from occurring. Essentially, a boxer's fracture occurs when the small metacarpal bone bends downward and toward the palm of the hand during impact with an extremely hard surface (such as a brick wall or human skull).

Wrist and Forearm Alignment

If you want to avoid injuring your wrists, you must always keep your wrists aligned with your forearm throughout the execution of your punch. This applies to both linear punches (lead straight, rear cross) as well as circular punches (hooks, uppercuts and shovel hooks).

If your wrist bends or collapses on impact, you will either sprain or break it. It's that simple. Remember, a sprained or broken wrist can cost you your life in a life-threatening self-defense situation. Also, don't make the false assumption that a fist loading device will keep your wrists straight. It won't.

If you want to avoid breaking or spraining your wrists, you must always remember to keep your wrists aligned with your forearm when punching.

Survival Weapons

One of the best ways to learn how to throw a punch without bending your wrists is to regularly workout on the heavy bag. The heavy bag will provide the necessary amount of resistance to strengthen and condition the bones, tendons, and ligaments in your wrists. Just remember to start off slowly and gradually increase the force of your punches.

Strong Hands, Wrists and Forearms

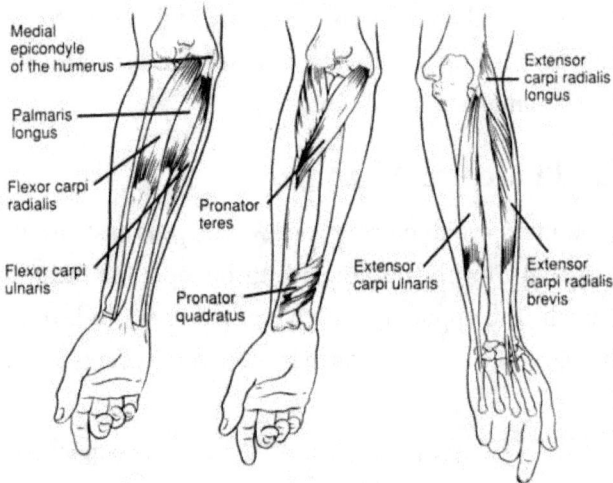

Medial
epicondyle
of the humerus

Palmaris
longus

Flexor carpi
radialis

Flexor carpi
ulnaris

Pronator
teres

Pronator
quadratus

Extensor
carpi ulnaris

Extensor
carpi radialis
longus

Extensor
carpi radialis
brevis

Proper fist configuration and wrist alignment are critical, but that's only half of the equation. You must have strong hands, wrists, and forearms to withstand the actual force of hitting with a fist loader.

You will, therefore, need to perform specific hand and forearm exercises to strengthen these muscles. Bruce Lee was well aware of this important fact. In fact, he would religiously strengthen his hands and forearms for the rigors of power punching. Lee knew that powerful and injury free punching relies heavily on the overall strength and structural integrity of your hands, wrists, and forearms.

132

Conditioning and Strength Training

There are many ways of strengthening your hands, wrists, and forearms for fist loaded punching. If you are low on cash and just starting out, you can begin by squeezing a tennis ball a couple of times per week. One hundred repetitions per hand would be a good start.

Power Putty

Later on you can add power putty to your hand strengthening routine. This unique hand exerciser is made up of silicone rubber that can be squeezed, pulled, pinched, clawed and stretched in just about any conceivable direction. This tough, resistant putty will strengthen the muscles of your forearm, wrists, hands, and fingers.

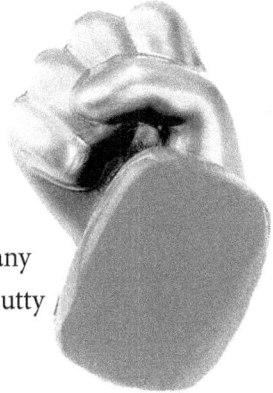

Hand Grippers

Another quick and effective way to strengthen your hands, wrists, and forearms is to work out with heavy duty hand grippers. While there is a wide selection of grippers on the market, I prefer the Captains of Crush brand. These high-quality grippers are virtually indestructible, and they come in a variety of different resistance levels ranging from 60 to 365 pounds.

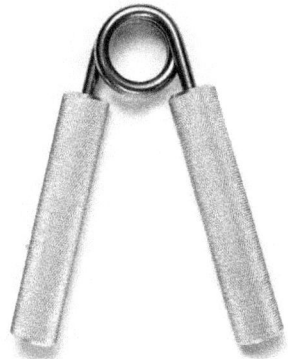

Weight Training

Finally, you can condition your wrists and forearms by performing various forearm exercises with free weights. Exercises like hammer curls, reverse curls, wrist curls, and reverse wrist curls are great for developing strong wrists, forearms, and hands. When training your forearms, be sure to work both your extensor and flexor muscles. Here are a few to get you started:

Barbell Wrist Curls

This exercise strengthens the flexor muscles. Perform 5 sets of 8-10 repetitions. To perform the exercise, follow these steps:

1. Sit at the end of a bench, grab a barbell with an underhand grip and place both of your hands close together.

2. In a smooth and controlled fashion, slowly bend your wrists and lower the barbell toward the floor.

3. Contract your forearms and curl the weight back to the starting position.

Reverse Wrist Curls

This exercise develops and strengthens the extensor muscle of the forearm. Perform 6 sets of 6-8 repetitions. To perform the exercise, follow these steps:

1. Sit at the end of a bench, hold a barbell with an overhand grip (your hands should be approximately 11 inches apart) and place your forearms on top of your thighs.

2. Slowly lower the barbell as far as your wrists will allow.

3. Flex your wrists upward back to the starting position.

Behind-the-Back Wrist Curls

This exercise strengthens both the flexor muscles of the forearms. Perform 5 sets of 6-8 repetitions To perform the exercise, follow these steps:

1. Hold a barbell behind your back at arm's length (your hands

should be approximately shoulder-width apart).

2. Uncurl your finger and let the barbell slowly roll down your palms.

3. Close your hands and roll the barbell back into your hands.

Hammer Curls

This exercise strengthens both the Brachialis and Brachioradialis muscles. Perform 5 sets of 8-10 repetitions. To perform the exercise, follow these steps:

1. Stand with both feet approximately shoulder-width apart, with both dumbbells at your sides.

2. Keeping your elbows close to your body and your palms facing inward, slowly curl both dumbbells upward towards your shoulders.

3. Slowly return to the starting position.

Reverse Barbell Curls

Reverse curls can be a great alternative to hammer curls. This exercise strengthens both the Brachialis and Brachioradialis muscles. Perform 5 sets of 8-10 repetitions. To perform the exercise, follow these steps:

1. Stand with both feet approximately shoulder width apart. Hold a barbell with your palms facing down (pronated grip).

2. Keeping your upper arms stationary, curl the weights up until the bar is at shoulder level.

3. Slowly return to the starting position.

Accuracy Counts!

The final component of injury free punching is target accuracy. For example, in a real world self-defense encounter, you must avoid hitting hard body surfaces like the opponent's skull.

Believe it or not, many self-defense hand injuries are a result of striking the opponent's skull, which is extremely hard and resilient. In many ways, it's likened to a crash helmet that protects the human brain from head injuries. I know several fighters who broke their hands when their fists connected with an opponent's forehead or skull during combat.

The bottom line is, you must be careful where you place your punches. It's important that your strikes are accurate, and your punches are timed correctly. This can be especially challenging considering that human targets move in unpredictable directions. Just keep in mind that one misplaced power punch can easily sprain or break your wrist.

Be Aware of What You Are Doing!

Learning how to punch correctly also means you will have to study and observe each punch in your arsenal and make certain they can handle the rigors of fist loading. Through proper analytical observation, you can quickly identify the strengths and weaknesses of each punch in your arsenal. The best way to accomplish this is to methodically test each punch on a heavy bag.

For example, take the most basic punch known to man - the rear cross. Begin by standing approximately four to five feet from the bag. Then, assume a fighting stance with your left leg forward and your body positioned at a forty-five degree angle from the bag. Make certain both of your hands are properly clenched into fists, and your head and chin are angled slightly down.

Now, deliver the punch, exhale and quickly twist and throw your rear arm and shoulder forward and towards the heavy bag. Make certain to twist your rear leg, hip, and shoulder forward and extend your rear arm straight. Do not lock out your rear arm when throwing the punch, be certain there is a slight bend in the elbow. Your punch should forcefully snap into the bag and then return to the starting position.

After delivering the punch to the heavy bag, make the following important observations:

1. What was the overall feeling of the punch when you delivered it? Did it feel rigid and forced or was it loose and fluid?

2. What happened when your punch connected with the bag? Did the punch snap or crack the heavy bag? Or did it just nudge it?

3. Did anything feel strained or hurt when your fist initially connected with the bag?

4. Was your punch accurate? Did you hit the bag exactly where you intended?

5. Did you remember to exhale or did you hold your breath when you threw the punch?

6. What happened to the structural integrity of your fist when you make contact with the punching bag? Did your fists open? Did your thumb get in the way? Did your wrist buckle inward?

7. Which knuckle made initial contact with the punching bag?

Finally, you might want to consider video taping yourself so you can quickly identify mistakes and errors in your punching form. Or perhaps you can have your training partner observe your punching technique and give you constructive feedback.

Chapter Eleven
Makeshift Weapons

Makeshift Weapons

When used correctly, that bandana can be an excellent makeshift weapon. However, before we get into the specifics, let take a closer look at the concept of a makeshift weapon. Essentially, makeshift weapons are common, everyday objects that can be converted into either offensive or defensive hand-held weapons.

A makeshift weapon must be appropriate to the function you have assigned to it. For instance, you won't be able to knock someone out with a car antennae, but you could whip it across their eyes and temporarily blind them. Whereas you could knock someone unconscious with a good heavy flashlight but you could not use it to shield yourself from a knife attack. Makeshift weapons can be broken down into the following four types:

- Cutting

- Shielding
- Distracting
- Striking

Cutting makeshift weapons

These are objects or implements used to stab or slash your assailant. Examples include:

- utility knive
- fork
- ice pick
- screwdriver
- broken glass
- straight razor
- pen
- pencil
- large nail
- ice scraper
- fire poker
- crow bar
- car keys
- pitch fork
- shovel
- hack saw
- knitting needle
- spike
- hatchet

Survival Weapons

- meat hook
- scissors
- letter opener
- cutting shears
- trowel

Shielding makeshift weapons

These are objects used to shield yourself from attack. Examples of shielding makeshift weapons include the following:

- briefcase
- trash-can lid
- bicycle
- thick sofa cushion
- backpack
- barstool
- lawn chair
- drawer
- cafeteria tray
- suitcase
- thick pillow
- leather jacket/coat
- sleeping bag
- motorcycle helmet
- small end table
- hubcap

Once again, be certain that your makeshift weapon has the

structural integrity to get the job done effectively.

Distracting makeshift weapons

These are objects that can be thrown into your assailant's face, torso, or legs to temporarily distract him. Generally distracting makeshift weapons are thrown into your assailant's face. Some examples include the following:

- sunglasses
- magazine
- car keys
- wallet
- ashtray
- heavy book
- salt shaker
- alarm clock
- coins
- bottle
- bars of soap
- shoe
- dirt
- sand
- gravel
- rock
- small figurine
- watering can
- hot liquids
- paperweight

Survival Weapons

- pesticide spray
- oven cleaner spray

A hot cup of coffee can be a great makeshift weapon.

Striking makeshift weapons

These are objects used to strike the assailant. Examples of striking makeshift weapons include some of the following examples:

- weighted bandana
- sticks
- brick
- crowbar
- baseball bat
- shovel
- golf club

- lamp
- heavy book
- light chair
- pool cue
- pipe
- heavy flashlight
- hammer
- binocular
- glass bottle
- beer mug
- tool box
- briefcase
- car door
- cane
- walking stick
- automobile
- motorcycle
- light dumbbells
- 2 x 4

Finally, there is some overlap between the various categories of make-shift weapons. For example, a briefcase can be thrown into an attacker's face for distraction, used to shield against a knife attack, or slammed into an assailant's temple to knock him out.

The Fighting Bandanna

A bandana is another great item you should add to your survival bag. This ubiquitous item is cheap, lightweight and has hundreds of practical uses. Most importantly, it makes a great striking makeshift weapon during an emergency self-defense situation.

For personal protection applications, the bandana can be quickly converted into an impact weapon, similar to a blackjack. This, of course will require a few quick modifications to the handkerchief. Similar to the fist loading concept, you'll want to add weight to the fabric which will amplify the impact power of your blow. Some practical and effective bandana loading objects include the following:

- *Metal Padlock*
- *Medium sized rock*
- *D-cell batteries*
- *Rolled coins (quarters or nickels are preferred)*
- *Cylindrical piece of metal*

- *Long spark plug socket*

Pictured here, a fighting bandana with a padlock.

Survival Weapons

Chapter Twelve
Last Ditch Weapons

The Fallacy of Dependency

Too many people assume that mere possession of a weapon will guarantee their safety during an emergency self-defense situation. This assumption forms the popular fallacy of dependency, the sole reliance on the particular weapon for personal protection. While a gun, tactical folder or other hand-held weapon will augment your personal protection, no single weapon is the definitive answer by itself.

All self-defense weapons have limitations. Consider, for example, the limitations of a hand gun. You can't take a handgun everywhere. Now I know what some of you are thinking: "I can conceal it in my bag." But that's not what I mean. Legal restrictions and disregard of the law aside, you still can't carry a handgun everywhere. If you don't take my word for it, try slipping one past airport security or into a courthouse.

But these aren't the only types of limitations. Criminals are smart. They usually rely on the element of surprise. They get the drop on you before you can get draw your gun. It happens all the time, even to police officers. Guns also jam, run out of ammunition, and misfire. Suffice it to say that knives pose even greater limitations. They can be dropped accidentally or taken away by a well seasoned criminal adversary. Knives also require close proximity to the attacker. Moreover, not all violent self-defense situations justify the use of a gun or a knife. Remember, when it comes to self-defense you have to be judge, jury and executioner all in a matter of seconds.

Natural Body Weapons - The Last Ditch Weapons

Therefore, if you want to be fully prepared to defend yourself and your loved ones against an assailant, you must also have a working knowledge of your natural body weapons. Body weapons are simply the various parts of your body that can be used immediately as weapons to neutralize a criminal attacker.

You have fourteen natural body weapons at your disposal. They are easy to learn and, when properly executed, have the potential to disable, cripple, and even kill an attacker. They include the head, teeth, voice, elbows, fists, palms, fingers and nails, edge of hand, web of the hand, knees, shins, dorsum of the foot, heel of foot, and ball of foot. Let's take a look at each one.

Head

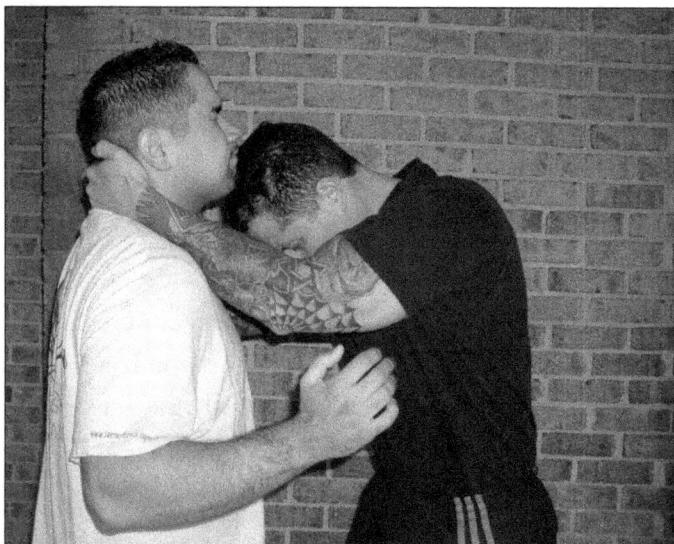

When you are fighting in close quarters, your head can be used for butting your assailant's nose. Head butts are ideal when a strong attacker has placed you in a hold where your arms are pinned against your sides.

Teeth

The teeth can be used for biting anything on the assailant's body (nose, ears, throat, fingers, etc.). It is important, however, for you to muster the mental determination to bite deep and hard into the assailant's flesh and shake your head vigorously, much like a vicious dog killing his enemy. While this may seem primitive and barbaric, it is essential to your survival.

Although a bite is extremely painful, it also transmits a strong psychological message to your assailant. It lets him know that you, too, can be vicious and are willing to do anything to survive the encounter.

Warning: There is one important concern to biting tactics: you run the risk of contracting AIDS if your attacker is infected and you draw blood while biting him.

Voice

Your voice is also a powerful weapon. When trained properly it can distract and startle your assailant, causing him to freeze temporarily.

Using Your Voice as a Survival Weapon

The voice can be a powerful weapon. When fighting back, the yell is a natural manifestation of the voice. The yell was probably part of earliest man's expressions. He undoubtedly used the yell in his life-and-death battles long before he learned the most basic forms of spoken language. The North American Indians were proficient in using the yell to strike fear in their enemies.

Yelling actually serves a strategic purpose in self-defense. Yelling while fighting back can distract, startle, and temporarily paralyze your assailant. It can cause him to freeze in his tracks, allowing you that split second advantage to deliver the first debilitating strike and thus to gain offensive control.

Yelling can also be used to psyche out the criminal. Imagine this situation: one minute you're talking calmly to a threatening aggressor and the next you are suddenly emitting a blood-curdling yell and striking him. This dramatic reversal can throw an assailant into a psychological tailspin.

Yelling also synchronizes your state of mind with the physical process taking place. It is the catalyst that sets off the killer instinct. It is the primal expression that harbors the killer instinct. In addition, yelling actually may draw attention to your emergency situation. In many cases, muggers, rapists, and street punks will abort their attacks and run to avoid detection.

You should work on developing a strong, powerful yell for self-defense. A good place to practice is in the privacy of your car. Its interior insulates you and amplifies your voice to give you a good idea of its power. Work on making your yell loud and ferocious, like a bear's or lion's. Let it rise from deep within your solar plexus. Practice prolonged yells and intermittent explosive ones. Finally, don't limit your yelling to raw primal sounds. Practice situational words like no, stop, hands off, and fire. Such words are ideal for a woman faced with a potential rapist.

Elbows

With very little training, you can learn to use your elbows as devastating self-defense weapons. They are explosive, deceptive, and difficult to stop. By rotating your body into the blow, you can generate tremendous force. You can deliver elbow strikes horizontally, vertically, and diagonally to the assailant's nose, temple, chin, throat, solar plexus, and ribs.

Fists

The fists are used for punching an assailant's temple, nose, chin, throat, solar plexus, ribs, and groin. However, punching with your fists is a true art, requiring considerable time and training to master. If your goal is short-term self-defense training, I suggest that you strike with the heel of your palm instead.

Warning: I also strongly recommend that women avoid punching with their fists. They generally have small hands and weak wrists and may have long nails, all of which can lead to broken wrists and fingers.

Survival Weapons

The Fingers/Nails

Your fingers and nails can be used for jabbing, gouging, and clawing a criminal's eyes. They can also be used for grabbing, pulling, tearing, and crushing his throat or testicles. To strengthen their fingernails, women should consider applying commercial nail-hardening liquid.

Palms

One alternative to punching with your fists is to strike with the heel of your palm. A palm strike from either one of your hands is very powerful and should always be delivered in an upward, thrusting motion to the assailant's nose or chin.

Edge of the Hand

You can throw the edge of your hand in a whiplike motion to surprise and neutralize your attacker. By whipping your arm horizontally to his nose or throat, you can cause severe injury or death. The edge of your hand can also be thrown vertically or diagonally to the back of the assailant's neck as a finishing blow.

Web of Hand

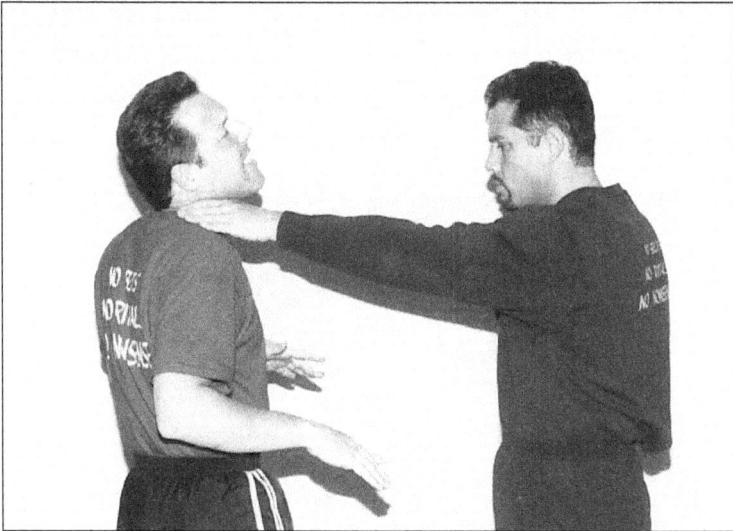

The web of your hand can be used to deliver web hand strikes to the opponent's throat. When striking, be certain to keep your hand stiff with your palm facing down.

Knees

When you are fighting a criminal in close-quarter grappling range, your knees can be extremely powerful weapons. You can deliver knee strikes vertically and diagonally to the assailant's thigh and groin, ribs, solar plexus, and face.

Shins

Striking with your shinbone can quickly cripple a powerful assailant and bring him to his knees in agony. That's right—your shinbone is a weapon. When striking with your shin, you can aim for his thigh, the side of his knee, or groin—and always remember to aim through your target.

Dorsum of Foot

You can use the dorsum of your foot to execute a vertical kick to the assailant's groin. Striking with the dorsum increases the power of your kick, prevents broken toes, and also lengthens the surface area of your strike.

Heel of the Foot

You can use the heel of your foot to execute a side kick to the criminal's knee or shin. When fighting an attacker in grappling range, you can use the heel of your foot to stomp down on the assailant's instep or toes.

Ball of the Foot

You can use the ball of your foot to execute a push kick into the assailant's thigh. You can also snap it quickly into the assailant's shin to loosen a grab from the front. When striking the assailant with the ball of your foot, be certain to pull your toes back to avoid jamming or breaking them.

Glossary

A

accuracy—The precise or exact projection of force. Accuracy is also defined as the ability to execute a combative movement with precision and exactness.

adaptability—The ability to physically and psychologically adjust to new or different conditions or circumstances of combat.

advanced first-strike tools—Offensive techniques that are specifically used when confronted with multiple opponents.

aerobic exercise—Literally, "with air." Exercise that elevates the heart rate to a training level for a prolonged period of time, usually 30 minutes.

affective preparedness – One of the three components of preparedness. Affective preparedness means being emotionally, philosophically, and spiritually prepared for the strains of combat. See cognitive preparedness and psychomotor preparedness.

aggression—Hostile and injurious behavior directed toward a person.

aggressive response—One of the three possible counters when assaulted by a grab, choke, or hold from a standing position. Aggressive response requires you to counter the enemy with destructive blows and strikes. See moderate response and passive response.

aggressive hand positioning—Placement of hands so as to imply aggressive or hostile intentions.

agility—An attribute of combat. One's ability to move his or her

Survival Weapons

body quickly and gracefully.

amalgamation—A scientific process of uniting or merging.

ambidextrous—The ability to perform with equal facility on both the right and left sides of the body.

anabolic steroids – synthetic chemical compounds that resemble the male sex hormone testosterone. This performance-enhancing drug is known to increase lean muscle mass, strength, and endurance.

analysis and integration—One of the five elements of CFA's mental component. This is the painstaking process of breaking down various elements, concepts, sciences, and disciplines into their atomic parts, and then methodically and strategically analyzing, experimenting, and drastically modifying the information so that it fulfills three combative requirements: efficiency, effectiveness, and safety. Only then is it finally integrated into the CFA system.

anatomical striking targets—The various anatomical body targets that can be struck and which are especially vulnerable to potential harm. They include: the eyes, temple, nose, chin, back of neck, front of neck, solar plexus, ribs, groin, thighs, knees, shins, and instep.

anchoring – The strategic process of trapping the assailant's neck or limb in order to control the range of engagement during razing.

assailant—A person who threatens or attacks another person.

assault—The threat or willful attempt to inflict injury upon the person of another.

assault and battery—The unlawful touching of another person without justification.

assessment—The process of rapidly gathering, analyzing, and accurately evaluating information in terms of threat and danger. You can assess people, places, actions, and objects.

attack—Offensive action designed to physically control, injure, or

166

kill another person.

attitude—One of the three factors that determine who wins a street fight. Attitude means being emotionally, philosophically, and spiritually liberated from societal and religious mores. See skills and knowledge.

attributes of combat—The physical, mental, and spiritual qualities that enhance combat skills and tactics.

awareness—Perception or knowledge of people, places, actions, and objects. (In CFA, there are three categories of tactical awareness: criminal awareness, situational awareness, and self-awareness.)

B

balance—One's ability to maintain equilibrium while stationary or moving.

blading the body—Strategically positioning your body at a 45-degree angle.

blitz and disengage—A style of sparring whereby a fighter moves into a range of combat, unleashes a strategic compound attack, and then quickly disengages to a safe distance. Of all sparring methodologies, the blitz and disengage most closely resembles a real street fight.

block—A defensive tool designed to intercept the assailant's attack by placing a non-vital target between the assailant's strike and your vital body target.

body composition—The ratio of fat to lean body tissue.

body language—Nonverbal communication through posture, gestures, and facial expressions.

body mechanics—Technically precise body movement during the execution of a body weapon, defensive technique, or other fighting maneuver.

body tackle – A tackle that occurs when your opponent haphazardly rushes forward and plows his body into yours.

body weapon—Also known as a tool, one of the various body parts that can be used to strike or otherwise injure or kill a criminal assailant.

burn out—A negative emotional state acquired by physically over- training. Some symptoms include: illness, boredom, anxiety, disinterest in training, and general sluggishness.

C

cadence—Coordinating tempo and rhythm to establish a timing pattern of movement.

cardiorespiratory conditioning—The component of physical fitness that deals with the heart, lungs, and circulatory system.

centerline—An imaginary vertical line that divides your body in half and which contains many of your vital anatomical targets.

choke holds—Holds that impair the flow of blood or oxygen to the brain.

circular movements—Movements that follow the direction of a curve.

close-quarter combat—One of the three ranges of knife and bludgeon combat. At this distance, you can strike, slash, or stab your assailant with a variety of close-quarter techniques.

cognitive development—One of the five elements of CFA's mental component. The process of developing and enhancing your fighting skills through specific mental exercises and techniques. See analysis and integration, killer instinct, philosophy, and strategic/tactical development.

cognitive exercises—Various mental exercises used to enhance fighting skills and tactics.

cognitive preparedness – One of the three components of preparedness. Cognitive preparedness means being equipped with the strategic concepts, principles, and general knowledge of combat. See affective preparedness and psychomotor preparedness.

combat-oriented training—Training that is specifically related to the harsh realities of both armed and unarmed combat. See ritual-oriented training and sport-oriented training.

combative arts—The various arts of war. See martial arts.

combative attributes—See attributes of combat.

combative fitness—A state characterized by cardiorespiratory and muscular/skeletal conditioning, as well as proper body composition.

combative mentality—Also known as the killer instinct, this is a combative state of mind necessary for fighting. See killer instinct.

combat ranges—The various ranges of unarmed combat.

combative utility—The quality of condition of being combatively useful.

combination(s)—See compound attack.

common peroneal nerve—A pressure point area located approximately four to six inches above the knee on the midline of the outside of the thigh.

composure—A combative attribute. Composure is a quiet and focused mind-set that enables you to acquire your combative agenda.

compound attack—One of the five conventional methods of attack. Two or more body weapons launched in strategic succession whereby the fighter overwhelms his assailant with a flurry of full speed, full-force blows.

conditioning training—A CFA training methodology requiring the practitioner to deliver a variety of offensive and defensive combinations for a 4-minute period. See proficiency training and street training.

contact evasion—Physically moving or manipulating your body to avoid being tackled by the adversary.

Contemporary Fighting Arts—A modern martial art and self-defense system made up of three parts: physical, mental, and spiritual.

conventional ground-fighting tools—Specific ground-fighting techniques designed to control, restrain, and temporarily incapacitate your adversary. Some conventional ground fighting tactics include: submission holds, locks, certain choking techniques, and specific striking techniques.

coordination—A physical attribute characterized by the ability to perform a technique or movement with efficiency, balance, and accuracy.

counterattack—Offensive action made to counter an assailant's initial attack.

courage—A combative attribute. The state of mind and spirit that enables a fighter to face danger and vicissitudes with confidence, resolution, and bravery.

creatine monohydrate—A tasteless and odorless white powder that mimics some of the effects of anabolic steroids. Creatine is a safe body-building product that can benefit anyone who wants to increase their strength, endurance, and lean muscle mass.

criminal awareness—One of the three categories of CFA awareness. It involves a general understanding and knowledge of the nature and dynamics of a criminal's motivations, mentalities, methods, and capabilities to perpetrate violent crime. See situational awareness and self-awareness.

criminal justice—The study of criminal law and the procedures associated with its enforcement.

criminology—The scientific study of crime and criminals.

cross-stepping—The process of crossing one foot in front of or behind the other when moving.

crushing tactics—Nuclear grappling-range techniques designed to crush the assailant's anatomical targets.

cue word - a unique word or personal statement that helps focus your attention on the execution of a skill, instead of its outcome.

D

deadly force—Weapons or techniques that may result in unconsciousness, permanent disfigurement, or death.

deception—A combative attribute. A stratagem whereby you delude your assailant.

decisiveness—A combative attribute. The ability to follow a tactical course of action that is unwavering and focused.

defense—The ability to strategically thwart an assailant's attack (armed or unarmed).

defensive flow—A progression of continuous defensive responses.

defensive mentality—A defensive mind-set.

defensive reaction time—The elapsed time between an assailant's physical attack and your defensive response to that attack. See offensive reaction time.

demeanor—A person's outward behavior. One of the essential factors to consider when assessing a threatening individual.

diet—A lifestyle of healthy eating.

disingenuous vocalization—The strategic and deceptive

utilization of words to successfully launch a preemptive strike at your adversary.

distancing—The ability to quickly understand spatial relationships and how they relate to combat.

distractionary tactics—Various verbal and physical tactics designed to distract your adversary.

double end bag—A small bag hung from the ceiling and anchored to the floor with two elastic cords. This unique training bag develops striking accuracy, speed, fighting rhythm, timing, eye-hand coordination, footwork and overall defensive skills.

double-leg takedown—A takedown that occurs when your opponent shoots for both of your legs to force you to the ground.

E

ectomorph—One of the three somatotypes. A body type characterized by a high degree of slenderness, angularity, and fragility. See endomorph and mesomorph.

effectiveness—One of the three criteria for a CFA body weapon, technique, tactic, or maneuver. It means the ability to produce a desired effect. See efficiency and safety.

efficiency—One of the three criteria for a CFA body weapon, technique, tactic, or maneuver. It means the ability to reach an objective quickly and economically. See effectiveness and safety.

emotionless—A combative attribute. Being temporarily devoid of human feeling.

endomorph—One of the three somatotypes. A body type characterized by a high degree of roundness, softness, and body fat. See ectomorph and mesomorph.

evasion—A defensive maneuver that allows you to strategically maneuver your body away from the assailant's strike.

evasive sidestepping—Evasive footwork where the practitioner moves to either the right or left side.

evasiveness—A combative attribute. The ability to avoid threat or danger.

excessive force—An amount of force that exceeds the need for a particular event and is unjustified in the eyes of the law.

experimentation—The painstaking process of testing a combative hypothesis or theory.

explosiveness—A combative attribute that is characterized by a sudden outburst of violent energy.

F

fear—A strong and unpleasant emotion caused by the anticipation or awareness of threat or danger. There are three stages of fear in order of intensity: fright, panic, and terror. See fright, panic, and terror.

feeder—A skilled technician who manipulates the focus mitts.

femoral nerve—A pressure point area located approximately 6 inches above the knee on the inside of the thigh.

fighting stance—Any one of the stances used in CFA's system. A strategic posture you can assume when face-to-face with an unarmed assailant(s). The fighting stance is generally used after you have launched your first-strike tool.

fight-or-flight syndrome—A response of the sympathetic nervous system to a fearful and threatening situation, during which it prepares your body to either fight or flee from the perceived danger.

finesse—A combative attribute. The ability to skillfully execute a movement or a series of movements with grace and refinement.

first strike—Proactive force used to interrupt the initial stages of an assault before it becomes a self-defense situation.

first-strike principle—A CFA principle that states that when physical danger is imminent and you have no other tactical option but to fight back, you should strike first, strike fast, and strike with authority and keep the pressure on.

first-strike stance—One of the stances used in CFA's system. A strategic posture used prior to initiating a first strike.

first-strike tools—Specific offensive tools designed to initiate a preemptive strike against your adversary.

fisted blows – Hand blows delivered with a clenched fist.

five tactical options – The five strategic responses you can make in a self-defense situation, listed in order of increasing level of resistance: comply, escape, de-escalate, assert, and fight back.

flexibility—The muscles' ability to move through maximum natural ranges. See muscular/skeletal conditioning.

focus mitts—Durable leather hand mitts used to develop and sharpen offensive and defensive skills.

footwork—Quick, economical steps performed on the balls of the feet while you are relaxed, alert, and balanced. Footwork is structured around four general movements: forward, backward, right, and left.

fractal tool—Offensive or defensive tools that can be used in more than one combat range.

fright—The first stage of fear; quick and sudden fear. See panic and terror.

full Beat – One of the four beat classifications in the Widow Maker Program. The full beat strike has a complete initiation and retraction phase.

G

going postal - a slang term referring to a person who suddenly and unexpectedly attacks you with an explosive and frenzied flurry of blows. Also known as postal attack.

grappling range—One of the three ranges of unarmed combat. Grappling range is the closest distance of unarmed combat from which you can employ a wide variety of close-quarter tools and techniques. The grappling range of unarmed combat is also divided into two planes: vertical (standing) and horizontal (ground fighting). See kicking range and punching range.

grappling-range tools—The various body tools and techniques that are employed in the grappling range of unarmed combat, including head butts; biting, tearing, clawing, crushing, and gouging tactics; foot stomps, horizontal, vertical, and diagonal elbow strikes, vertical and diagonal knee strikes, chokes, strangles, joint locks, and holds. See punching range tools and kicking range tools.

ground fighting—Also known as the horizontal grappling plane, this is fighting that takes place on the ground.

guard—Also known as the hand guard, this refers to a fighter's hand positioning.

guard position—Also known as leg guard or scissors hold, this is a ground-fighting position in which a fighter is on his back holding his opponent between his legs.

H

half beat - One of the four beat classifications in the Widow Maker Program. The half beat strike is delivered through the retraction phase of the proceeding strike.

hand positioning—See guard.

hand wraps—Long strips of cotton that are wrapped around the hands and wrists for greater protection.

haymaker—A wild and telegraphed swing of the arms executed by an unskilled fighter.

head-hunter—A fighter who primarily attacks the head.

heavy bag—A large cylindrical bag used to develop kicking, punching, or striking power.

high-line kick—One of the two different classifications of a kick. A kick that is directed to targets above an assailant's waist level. See low-line kick.

hip fusing—A full-contact drill that teaches a fighter to "stand his ground" and overcome the fear of exchanging blows with a stronger opponent. This exercise is performed by connecting two fighters with a 3-foot chain, forcing them to fight in the punching range of unarmed combat.

histrionics—The field of theatrics or acting.

hook kick—A circular kick that can be delivered in both kicking and punching ranges.

hook punch—A circular punch that can be delivered in both the punching and grappling ranges.

I

impact power—Destructive force generated by mass and velocity.

impact training—A training exercise that develops pain tolerance.

incapacitate—To disable an assailant by rendering him unconscious or damaging his bones, joints, or organs.

initiative—Making the first offensive move in combat.

inside position—The area between the opponent's arms, where he has the greatest amount of control.

intent—One of the essential factors to consider when assessing a threatening individual. The assailant's purpose or motive. See demeanor, positioning, range, and weapon capability.

intuition—The innate ability to know or sense something without the use of rational thought.

J

jersey Pull – Strategically pulling the assailant's shirt or jacket over his head as he disengages from the clinch position.

joint lock—A grappling-range technique that immobilizes the assailant's joint.

K

kick—A sudden, forceful strike with the foot.

kicking range—One of the three ranges of unarmed combat. Kicking range is the furthest distance of unarmed combat wherein you use your legs to strike an assailant. See grappling range and punching range.

kicking-range tools—The various body weapons employed in the kicking range of unarmed combat, including side kicks, push kicks, hook kicks, and vertical kicks.

killer instinct—A cold, primal mentality that surges to your consciousness and turns you into a vicious fighter.

kinesics—The study of nonlinguistic body movement communications. (For example, eye movement, shrugs, or facial gestures.)

kinesiology—The study of principles and mechanics of human movement.

kinesthetic perception—The ability to accurately feel your body during the execution of a particular movement.

knowledge—One of the three factors that determine who will win a street fight. Knowledge means knowing and understanding how to fight. See skills and attitude.

L

lead side -The side of the body that faces an assailant.

leg guard—See guard position.

linear movement—Movements that follow the path of a straight line.

low-maintenance tool—Offensive and defensive tools that require the least amount of training and practice to maintain proficiency. Low maintenance tools generally do not require preliminary stretching.

low-line kick—One of the two different classifications of a kick. A kick that is directed to targets below the assailant's waist level. (See high-line kick.)

lock—See joint lock.

M

maneuver—To manipulate into a strategically desired position.

MAP—An acronym that stands for moderate, aggressive, passive. MAP provides the practitioner with three possible responses to various grabs, chokes, and holds that occur from a standing position. See aggressive response, moderate response, and passive response.

Marathon des Sables (MdS) - a six-day, 156-mile ultramarathon held in southern Morocco, in the Sahara Desert. It is considered by many to be the toughest footrace on earth.

martial arts—The "arts of war."

masking—The process of concealing your true feelings from your opponent by manipulating and managing your body language.

mechanics—(See body mechanics.)

mental toughness - a performance mechanism utilizing a collection of mental attributes that allow a person to cope, perform and prevail through the stress of extreme adversity.

mental component—One of the three vital components of the CFA system. The mental component includes the cerebral aspects of fighting including the killer instinct, strategic and tactical development, analysis and integration, philosophy, and cognitive development. See physical component and spiritual component.

mesomorph—One of the three somatotypes. A body type classified by a high degree of muscularity and strength. The mesomorph possesses the ideal physique for unarmed combat. See ectomorph and endomorph.

mobility—A combative attribute. The ability to move your body quickly and freely while balanced. See footwork.

moderate response—One of the three possible counters when assaulted by a grab, choke, or hold from a standing position. Moderate response requires you to counter your opponent with a control and restraint (submission hold). See aggressive response and passive response.

modern martial art—A pragmatic combat art that has evolved to meet the demands and characteristics of the present time.

mounted position—A dominant ground-fighting position where a fighter straddles his opponent.

muscular endurance—The muscles' ability to perform the same

motion or task repeatedly for a prolonged period of time.

muscular flexibility—The muscles' ability to move through maximum natural ranges.

muscular strength—The maximum force that can be exerted by a particular muscle or muscle group against resistance.

muscular/skeletal conditioning—An element of physical fitness that entails muscular strength, endurance, and flexibility.

N

naked choke—A throat choke executed from the chest to back position. This secure choke is executed with two hands and it can be performed while standing, kneeling, and ground fighting with the opponent.

neck crush – A powerful pain compliance technique used when the adversary buries his head in your chest to avoid being razed.

neutralize—See incapacitate.

neutral zone—The distance outside the kicking range at which neither the practitioner nor the assailant can touch the other.

nonaggressive physiology—Strategic body language used prior to initiating a first strike.

nontelegraphic movement—Body mechanics or movements that do not inform an assailant of your intentions.

nuclear ground-fighting tools—Specific grappling range tools designed to inflict immediate and irreversible damage. Nuclear tools and tactics include biting tactics, tearing tactics, crushing tactics, continuous choking tactics, gouging techniques, raking tactics, and all striking techniques.

O

offense—The armed and unarmed means and methods of attacking a criminal assailant.

offensive flow—Continuous offensive movements (kicks, blows, and strikes) with unbroken continuity that ultimately neutralize or terminate the opponent. See compound attack.

offensive reaction time—The elapsed time between target selection and target impaction.

one-mindedness—A state of deep concentration wherein you are free from all distractions (internal and external).

ostrich defense—One of the biggest mistakes one can make when defending against an opponent. This is when the practitioner looks away from that which he fears (punches, kicks, and strikes). His mentality is, "If I can't see it, it can't hurt me."

P

pain tolerance—Your ability to physically and psychologically withstand pain.

panic—The second stage of fear; overpowering fear. See fright and terror.

parry—A defensive technique: a quick, forceful slap that redirects an assailant's linear attack. There are two types of parries: horizontal and vertical.

passive response—One of the three possible counters when assaulted by a grab, choke, or hold from a standing position. Passive response requires you to nullify the assault without injuring your adversary. See aggressive response and moderate response.

patience—A combative attribute. The ability to endure and

tolerate difficulty.

perception—Interpretation of vital information acquired from your senses when faced with a potentially threatening situation.

philosophical resolution—The act of analyzing and answering various questions concerning the use of violence in defense of yourself and others.

philosophy—One of the five aspects of CFA's mental component. A deep state of introspection whereby you methodically resolve critical questions concerning the use of force in defense of yourself or others.

physical attributes—The numerous physical qualities that enhance your combative skills and abilities.

physical component—One of the three vital components of the CFA system. The physical component includes the physical aspects of fighting, such as physical fitness, weapon/technique mastery, and combative attributes. See mental component and spiritual component.

physical conditioning—See combative fitness.

physical fitness—See combative fitness.

positional asphyxia—The arrangement, placement, or positioning of your opponent's body in such a way as to interrupt your breathing and cause unconsciousness or possibly death.

positioning—The spatial relationship of the assailant to the assailed person in terms of target exposure, escape, angle of attack, and various other strategic considerations.

postal attack - see going postal.

power—A physical attribute of armed and unarmed combat. The amount of force you can generate when striking an anatomical target.

power generators—Specific points on your body that generate

impact power. There are three anatomical power generators: shoulders, hips, and feet.

precision—See accuracy.

preemptive strike—See first strike.

premise—An axiom, concept, rule, or any other valid reason to modify or go beyond that which has been established.

preparedness—A state of being ready for combat. There are three components of preparedness: affective preparedness, cognitive preparedness, and psychomotor preparedness.

probable reaction dynamics - The opponent's anticipated or predicted movements or actions during both armed and unarmed combat.

proficiency training—A CFA training methodology requiring the practitioner to execute a specific body weapon, technique, maneuver, or tactic over and over for a prescribed number of repetitions. See conditioning training and street training.

proxemics—The study of the nature and effect of man's personal space.

proximity—The ability to maintain a strategically safe distance from a threatening individual.

pseudospeciation—A combative attribute. The tendency to assign subhuman and inferior qualities to a threatening assailant.

psychological conditioning—The process of conditioning the mind for the horrors and rigors of real combat.

psychomotor preparedness—One of the three components of preparedness. Psychomotor preparedness means possessing all of the physical skills and attributes necessary to defeat a formidable adversary. See affective preparedness and cognitive preparedness.

punch—A quick, forceful strike of the fists.

punching range—One of the three ranges of unarmed combat. Punching range is the mid range of unarmed combat from which the fighter uses his hands to strike his assailant. See kicking range and grappling range.

punching-range tools—The various body weapons that are employed in the punching range of unarmed combat, including finger jabs, palm-heel strikes, rear cross, knife-hand strikes, horizontal and shovel hooks, uppercuts, and hammer-fist strikes. See grappling-range tools and kicking-range tools.

Q

qualities of combat—See attributes of combat.

quarter beat - One of the four beat classifications of the Widow Maker Program. Quarter beat strikes never break contact with the assailant's face. Quarter beat strikes are primarily responsible for creating the psychological panic and trauma when Razing.

R

range—The spatial relationship between a fighter and a threatening assailant.

range deficiency—The inability to effectively fight and defend in all ranges of combat (armed and unarmed).

range manipulation—A combative attribute. The strategic manipulation of combat ranges.

range proficiency—A combative attribute. The ability to effectively fight and defend in all ranges of combat (armed and unarmed).

ranges of engagement—See combat ranges.

ranges of unarmed combat—The three distances (kicking range, punching range, and grappling range) a fighter might physically engage with an assailant while involved in unarmed combat.

raze – To level, demolish or obliterate.

razer – One who performs the Razing methodology.

razing – The second phase of the Widow Maker Program. A series of vicious close quarter techniques designed to physically and psychologically extirpate a criminal attacker.

razing amplifier - a technique, tactic or procedure that magnifies the destructiveness of your razing technique.

reaction dynamics—see probable reaction dynamics.

reaction time—The elapsed time between a stimulus and the response to that particular stimulus. See offensive reaction time and defensive reaction time.

rear cross—A straight punch delivered from the rear hand that crosses from right to left (if in a left stance) or left to right (if in a right stance).

rear side—The side of the body furthest from the assailant. See lead side.

reasonable force—That degree of force which is not excessive for a particular event and which is appropriate in protecting yourself or others.

refinement—The strategic and methodical process of improving or perfecting.

relocation principle—Also known as relocating, this is a street-fighting tactic that requires you to immediately move to a new location (usually by flanking your adversary) after delivering a compound attack.

repetition—Performing a single movement, exercise, strike, or action continuously for a specific period.

research—A scientific investigation or inquiry.

rhythm—Movements characterized by the natural ebb and flow of related elements.

ritual-oriented training—Formalized training that is conducted without intrinsic purpose. See combat-oriented training and sport-oriented training.

S

safety—One of the three criteria for a CFA body weapon, technique, maneuver, or tactic. It means that the tool, technique, maneuver or tactic provides the least amount of danger and risk for the practitioner. See efficiency and effectiveness.

scissors hold—See guard position.

scorching – Quickly and inconspicuously applying oleoresin capsicum (hot pepper extract) on your fingertips and then razing your adversary.

self-awareness—One of the three categories of CFA awareness. Knowing and understanding yourself. This includes aspects of yourself which may provoke criminal violence and which will promote a proper and strong reaction to an attack. See criminal awareness and situational awareness.

self-confidence—Having trust and faith in yourself.

self-enlightenment—The state of knowing your capabilities, limitations, character traits, feelings, general attributes, and motivations. See self-awareness.

set—A term used to describe a grouping of repetitions.

shadow fighting—A CFA training exercise used to develop and

refine your tools, techniques, and attributes of armed and unarmed combat.

sharking – A counter attack technique that is used when your adversary grabs your razing hand.

shielding wedge - a defensive maneuver used to counter an unarmed postal attack.

situational awareness—One of the three categories of CFA awareness. A state of being totally alert to your immediate surroundings, including people, places, objects, and actions. (See criminal awareness and self-awareness.)

skeletal alignment—The proper alignment or arrangement of your body. Skeletal alignment maximizes the structural integrity of striking tools.

skills—One of the three factors that determine who will win a street fight. Skills refers to psychomotor proficiency with the tools and techniques of combat. See Attitude and Knowledge.

slipping—A defensive maneuver that permits you to avoid an assailant's linear blow without stepping out of range. Slipping can be accomplished by quickly snapping the head and upper torso sideways (right or left) to avoid the blow.

snap back—A defensive maneuver that permits you to avoid an assailant's linear and circular blows without stepping out of range. The snap back can be accomplished by quickly snapping the head backward to avoid the assailant's blow.

somatotypes—A method of classifying human body types or builds into three different categories: endomorph, mesomorph, and ectomorph. See endomorph, mesomorph, and ectomorph.

sparring—A training exercise where two or more fighters fight each other while wearing protective equipment.

speed—A physical attribute of armed and unarmed combat. The rate or a measure of the rapid rate of motion.

spiritual component—One of the three vital components of the CFA system. The spiritual component includes the metaphysical issues and aspects of existence. See physical component and mental component.

sport-oriented training—Training that is geared for competition and governed by a set of rules. See combat-oriented training and ritual-oriented training.

sprawling—A grappling technique used to counter a double- or single-leg takedown.

square off—To be face-to-face with a hostile or threatening assailant who is about to attack you.

stance—One of the many strategic postures you assume prior to or during armed or unarmed combat.

stick fighting—Fighting that takes place with either one or two sticks.

strategic positioning—Tactically positioning yourself to either escape, move behind a barrier, or use a makeshift weapon.

strategic/tactical development—One of the five elements of CFA's mental component.

strategy—A carefully planned method of achieving your goal of engaging an assailant under advantageous conditions.

street fight—A spontaneous and violent confrontation between two or more individuals wherein no rules apply.

street fighter—An unorthodox combatant who has no formal training. His combative skills and tactics are usually developed in the street by the process of trial and error.

street training—A CFA training methodology requiring the

practitioner to deliver explosive compound attacks for 10 to 20 seconds. See condition ng training and proficiency training.

strength training—The process of developing muscular strength through systematic application of progressive resistance.

stress - physiological and psychological arousal caused by a stressor.

stressors - any activity, situation, circumstance, event, experience, or condition that causes a person to experience both physiological and psychological stress.

striking art—A combat art that relies predominantly on striking techniques to neutralize or terminate a criminal attacker.

striking shield—A rectangular shield constructed of foam and vinyl used to develop power in your kicks, punches, and strikes.

striking tool—A natural body weapon that impacts with the assailant's anatomical target.

strong side—The strongest and most coordinated side of your body.

style—The distinct manner in which a fighter executes or performs his combat skills.

stylistic integration—The purposeful and scientific collection of tools and techniques from various disciplines, which are strategically integrated and dramatically altered to meet three essential criteria: efficiency, effectiveness, and combative safety.

submission holds—Also known as control and restraint techniques, many of these locks and holds create sufficient pain to cause the adversary to submit.

sucker punch—Proactive force used to interrupt the initial stages of an assault before it becomes a self-defense situation. (See first strike.)

system—The unification of principles, philosophies, rules, strategies, methodologies, tools, and techniques of a particular method of combat.

T

tactic—The skill of using the available means to achieve an end.

target awareness—A combative attribute that encompasses five strategic principles: target orientation, target recognition, target selection, target impaction, and target exploitation.

target exploitation—A combative attribute. The strategic maximization of your assailant's reaction dynamics during a fight. Target exploitation can be applied in both armed and unarmed encounters.

target impaction—The successful striking of the appropriate anatomical target.

target orientation—A combative attribute. Having a workable knowledge of the assailant's anatomical targets.

target recognition—The ability to immediately recognize appropriate anatomical targets during an emergency self-defense situation.

target selection—The process of mentally selecting the appropriate anatomical target for your self-defense situation. This is predicated on certain factors, including proper force response, assailant's positioning, and range.

target stare—A form of telegraphing in which you stare at the anatomical target you intend to strike.

target zones—The three areas in which an assailant's anatomical targets are located. (See zone one, zone two and zone three.)

technique—A systematic procedure by which a task is

accomplished.

telegraphic cognizance—A combative attribute. The ability to recognize both verbal and non-verbal signs of aggression or assault.

telegraphing—Unintentionally making your intentions known to your adversary.

tempo—The speed or rate at which you speak.

terminate—To kill.

terror—The third stage of fear; defined as overpowering fear. See fright and panic.

timing—A physical and mental attribute of armed and unarmed combat. Your ability to execute a movement at the optimum moment.

tone—The overall quality or character of your voice.

tool—See body weapon.

traditional martial arts—Any martial art that fails to evolve and change to meet the demands and characteristics of its present environment.

traditional style/system—See traditional martial arts.

training drills—The various exercises and drills aimed at perfecting combat skills, attributes, and tactics.

trap and tuck – A counter move technique used when the adversary attempts to raze you during your quarter beat assault.

U

unified mind—A mind free and clear of distractions and focused on the combative situation.

use of force response—A combative attribute. Selecting the appropriate level of force for a particular self-defense situation.

V

viciousness—A combative attribute. The propensity to be extremely violent and destructive often characterized by intense savagery.

violence—The intentional utilization of physical force to coerce, injure, cripple, or kill.

visualization—Also known as mental visualization or mental imagery. The purposeful formation of mental images and scenarios in the mind's eye.

W

warm-up—A series of mild exercises, stretches, and movements designed to prepare you for more intense exercise.

weak side—The weaker and more uncoordinated side of your body.

weapon and technique mastery—A component of CFA's physical component. The kinesthetic and psychomotor development of a weapon or combative technique.

weapon capability—An assailant's ability to use and attack with a particular weapon.

webbing - The first phase of the Widow Maker Program. Webbing is a two hand strike delivered to the assailant's chin. It is called Webbing because your hands resemble a large web that wraps around the enemy's face.

widow maker – One who makes widows by destroying husbands.

widow maker program – A CFA combat program specifically designed to teach the law abiding citizen how to use extreme force when faced with immediate threat of unlawful deadly criminal attack. The Widow Maker program is divided into two phases or methodologies: Webbing and Razing.

Y

yell—A loud and aggressive scream or shout used for various strategic reasons.

Z

zero beat – One of the four beat classifications of the Widow Maker, Feral Fighting and Savage Street Fighting Programs. Zero beat strikes are full pressure techniques applied to a specific target until it completely ruptures. They include gouging, crushing, biting, and choking techniques.

zone one—Anatomical targets related to your senses, including the eyes, temple, nose, chin, and back of neck.

zone three—Anatomical targets related to your mobility, including thighs, knees, shins, and instep.

zone two—Anatomical targets related to your breathing, including front of neck, solar plexus, ribs, and groin.

About Sammy Franco

With over 30 years of experience, Sammy Franco is one of the world's foremost authorities on armed and unarmed self-defense. Highly regarded as a leading innovator in martial arts, Mr. Franco was one of the premier pioneers in the field of "reality-based" self-defense and combat instruction.

Sammy Franco is perhaps best known as the founder and creator of Contemporary Fighting Arts (CFA), a state-of-the-art offensive-based combat system that is specifically designed for real-world self-defense. CFA is a sophisticated and practical system of self-defense, designed specifically to provide efficient and effective methods to avoid, defuse, confront, and neutralize both armed and unarmed attackers.

Sammy Franco has frequently been featured in martial art magazines, newspapers, and appeared on numerous radio and television programs. Mr. Franco has also authored numerous books, magazine articles, and editorials and has developed a popular library of instructional videos.

Sammy Franco's experience and credibility in the combat science is unequaled. One of his many accomplishments in this field includes the fact that he has earned the ranking of a Law Enforcement Master Instructor, and has designed, implemented, and taught officer survival training to the United States Border Patrol (USBP). He has instructed members of the US Secret Service, Military Special Forces, Washington DC Police Department, Montgomery County, Maryland

Deputy Sheriffs, and the US Library of Congress Police. Sammy Franco is also a member of the prestigious International Law Enforcement Educators and Trainers Association (ILEETA) as well as the American Society of Law Enforcement Trainers (ASLET) and he is listed in the "Who's Who Director of Law Enforcement Instructors."

Sammy Franco is also a nationally certified Law Enforcement Instructor in the following curricula: PR-24 Side-Handle Baton, Police Arrest and Control Procedures, Police Personal Weapons Tactics, Police Power Handcuffing Methods, Police Oleoresin Capsicum Aerosol Training (OCAT), Police Weapon Retention and Disarming Methods, Police Edged Weapon Countermeasures and "Use of Force" Assessment and Response Methods.

Mr. Franco regularly conducts dynamic and enlightening seminars on different aspects of combat training, mental toughness and achieving personal peak performance.

On a personal level, Sammy Franco is an animal lover, who will go to great lengths to assist and rescue animals. Throughout the years, he's rescued everything from turkey vultures to goats. However, his most treasured moments are always spent with his beloved German Shepherd dogs.

For more information about Mr. Franco, you can visit his website at **SammyFranco.com** or follow him on Twitter **@RealSammyFranco**

Other Books by Sammy Franco

KUBOTAN POWER
Quick and Simple Steps to Mastering the Kubotan Keychain
by Sammy Franco

With over 290 photographs and step-by-step instructions, Kubotan Power is the authoritative resource for mastering this devastating self-defense weapon. In this one-of-a-kind book, world-renowned self-defense expert, Sammy Franco takes thirty years of real-world teaching experience and gives you quick, easy and practical kubotan techniques that can be used by civilians, law enforcement personnel, or military professionals. 8.5 x 5.5, paperback, 290 photos, illustrations, 204 pages.

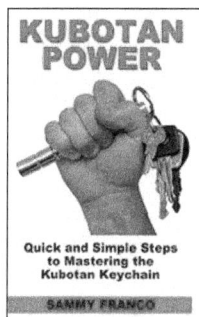

FIRST STRIKE
End a Fight in Ten Seconds or Less!
by Sammy Franco

Learn how to stop any attack before it starts by mastering the art of the preemptive strike. First Strike gives you an easy-to-learn yet highly effective self-defense game plan for handling violent close-quarter combat encounters. First Strike will teach you instinctive, practical and realistic self-defense techniques that will drop any criminal attacker to the floor with one punishing blow. By reading this book and by practicing, you will learn the hard-hitting skills necessary to execute a punishing first strike and ultimately prevail in a self-defense situation. 8.5 x 5.5, paperback, photos, illustrations, 202 pages.

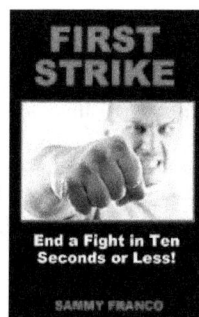

MAXIMUM DAMAGE
Hidden Secrets Behind Brutal Fighting Combination
by Sammy Franco

Maximum Damage teaches you the quickest ways to beat your opponent by exploiting his physical and psychological reactions in a fight. Learn how to stay two steps ahead of your adversary by knowing exactly how he will react to your strikes before they are delivered. In this unique book, self-defense expert Sammy Franco reveals his unique Probable Reaction Dynamic (PRD) fighting method. Probable reaction dynamics are both a scientific and comprehensive offensive strategy based on the positional theory of combat. Regardless of your style of fighting, PRD training will help you overpower your opponent by integrating your strikes into brutal fighting combinations that are fast, ferocious and final! 8.5 x 5.5, paperback, 240 photos, illustrations, 238 pages.

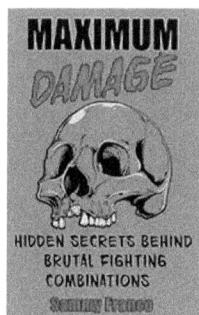

HEAVY BAG TRAINING
For Boxing, Mixed Martial Arts and Self-Defense
(Heavy Bag Training Series Book 1)
by Sammy Franco

The heavy bag is one of the oldest and most recognizable pieces of training equipment. It's used by boxers, mixed martial artists, self-defense practitioners, and fitness enthusiasts. Unfortunately, most people don't know how to use the heavy bag correctly. Heavy Bag Training teaches you everything you ever wanted to know about working out on the heavy bag. In this one-of-a-kind book, world-renowned self-defense expert Sammy Franco provides you with the knowledge, skills, and attitude necessary to maximize the training benefits of the bag. 8.5 x 5.5, paperback, photos, illus, 172 pages.

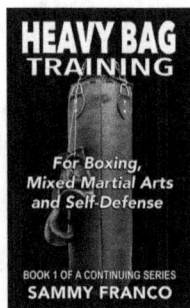

HEAVY BAG COMBINATIONS
The Ultimate Guide to Heavy Bag Punching Combinations
(Heavy Bag Training Series Book 2)
by Sammy Franco

Heavy Bag Combinations is the second book in Sammy Franco's best-selling Heavy Bag Training Series. This unique book is your ultimate guide to mastering devastating heavy bag punching combinations. With over 300+ photographs and detailed step-by-step instructions, Heavy Bag Combinations provides beginner, intermediate and advanced heavy bag workout combinations that will challenge you for the rest of your life! In fact, even the most experienced athlete will advance his fighting skills to the next level and beyond. 8.5 x 5.5, paperback, photos, illus, 248 pages.

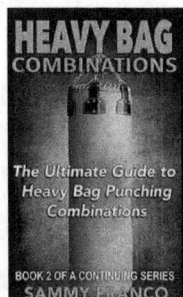

THE COMPLETE BODY OPPONENT BAG BOOK
by Sammy Franco

In this one-of-a-kind book, Sammy Franco teaches you the many hidden training features of the body opponent bag that will improve your fighting skills and boost your conditioning. With detailed photographs, step-by-step instructions, and dozens of unique workout routines, The Complete Body Opponent Bag Book is the authoritative resource for mastering this lifelike punching bag. It covers stances, punching, kicking, grappling techniques, mobility and footwork, targets, fighting ranges, training gear, time based workouts, punching and kicking combinations, weapons training, grappling drills, ground fighting, and dozens of workouts. 8.5 x 5.5, paperback, 139 photos, illustrations, 206 pages.

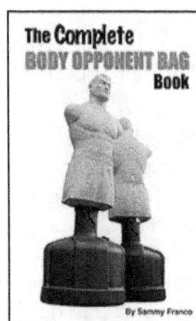

INVINCIBLE
Mental Toughness Techniques for the Street, Battlefield and Playing Field
by Sammy Franco

Invincible is a treasure trove of battle-tested techniques and strategies for improving mental toughness in all aspects of life. It teaches you how to unlock the true power of your mind and achieve success in sports, fitness, high-risk professions, self-defense, and other peak performance activities. However, you don't have to be an athlete or warrior to benefit from this unique mental toughness book. In fact, the mental skills featured in this indispensable program can be used by anyone who wants to reach their full potential in life. 8.5 x 5.5, paperback, photos, illus, 250 pages.

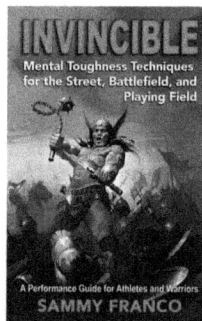

THE WIDOW MAKER PROGRAM
Extreme Self-Defense for Deadly Force Situations
by Sammy Franco

The Widow Maker Program is a shocking and revolutionary fighting style designed to unleash extreme force when faced with the immediate threat of an unlawful deadly criminal attack. In this unique book, self-defense innovator Sammy Franco teaches you his brutal and unorthodox combat style that is virtually indefensible and utterly devastating. With over 250 photographs and detailed step-by-step instructions, The Widow Maker Program teaches you Franco's surreptitious Webbing and Razing techniques. When combined, these two fighting methods create an unstoppable force capable of destroying the toughest adversary. 8.5 x 5.5, paperback, photos, illus, 218 pages.

FERAL FIGHTING
Advanced Widow Maker Fighting Techniques
by Sammy Franco

In this sequel, Sammy Franco marches forward with cutting-edge concepts and techniques that will take your self-defense skills to entirely new levels of combat performance. Feral Fighting includes Franco's revolutionary Shielding Wedge technique. When used correctly, it transforms you into an unstoppable human meat grinder, capable of destroying any criminal adversary. Feral Fighting also teaches you the cunning art or Scorching. Learn how to convert your fingertips into burning torches that generate over 2 million scoville heat units causing excruciating pain and temporarily blindness. 8.5 x 5.5, paperback, photos, illustrations, 204 pages.

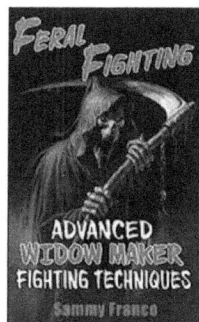

SAVAGE STREET FIGHTING
Tactical Savagery as a Last Resort
by Sammy Franco

In this revolutionary book, Sammy Franco reveals the science behind his most primal street fighting method. Savage Street Fighting is a brutal self-defense system specifically designed to teach the law-abiding citizen how to use "Tactical Savagery" when faced with the immediate threat of an unlawful deadly criminal attack. Savage Street Fighting is systematically engineered to protect you when there are no other self-defense options left! With over 300 photographs and detailed step-by-step instructions, Savage Street Fighting is a must-have book for anyone concerned about real world self-defense. Now is the time to learn how to unleash your inner beast! 8.5 x 5.5, paperback, 317 photos, illustrations, 232 pages.

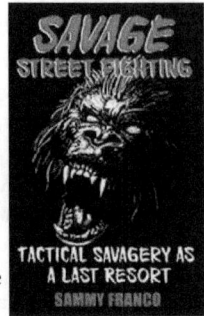

WAR MACHINE
How to Transform Yourself Into A Vicious & Deadly Street Fighter
by Sammy Franco

War Machine is a book that will change you for the rest of your life! When followed accordingly, War Machine will forge your mind, body and spirit into iron. Once armed with the mental and physical attributes of the War Machine, you will become a strong and confident warrior that can handle just about anything that life may throw your way. In essence, War Machine is a way of life. Powerful, intense, and hard. 11 x 8.5, paperback, photos, illustrations, 210 pages.